india

First published in 2003
Reprinted 2005.

Prakash Books India (P) Ltd.
1, Ansari Road, Darya Ganj,
New Delhi-110002
Ph.: 91-11-2324 3050-52 Fax: 91-11-2324 6975
E-mail: sales@prakashbooks.com
website: www.prakashbooks.com.

Designed by: Yogesh Suraksha Design Studio

Special thanks to Ravi Vyas, Richa Sharan, Anne Campbell,
Charanbir Oberoi, Sadhu Singh Saar, Archaeological Survey of India
and National Museum, New Delhi

ISBN: 81-7234-055-9

Printed and bound at Ajanta Offset & Packagings Ltd., New Delhi

india
exotic destination

tarun chopra

Prakash Books

contents

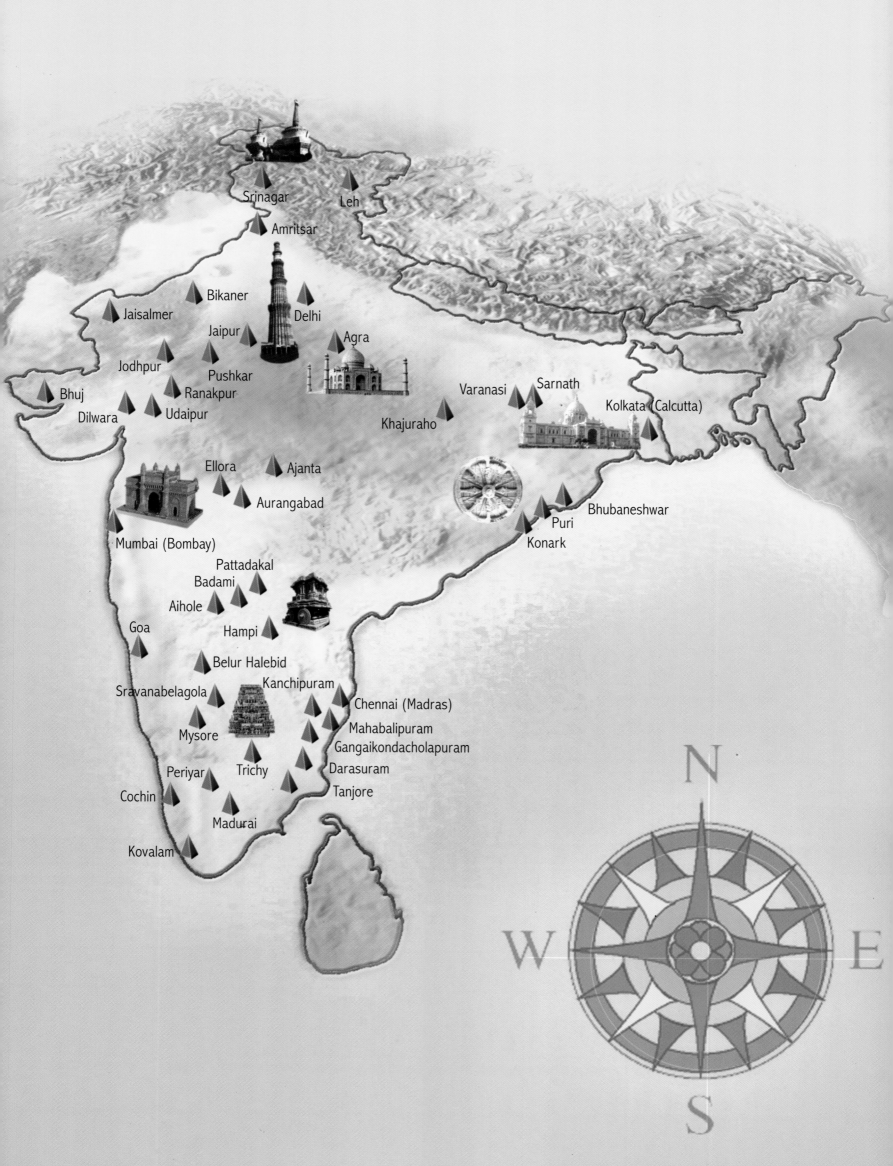

Srinagar

Leh

Amritsar

Bikaner

Jaisalmer

Delhi

Jaipur

Jodhpur

Pushkar

Bhuj

Ranakpur

Dilwara

Udaipur

Agra

Varanasi

Sarnath

Kolkata (Calcutta)

Khajuraho

Ellora

Ajanta

Aurangabad

Bhubaneshwar

Puri

Konark

Mumbai (Bombay)

Pattadakal

Badami

Aihole

Goa

Hampi

Belur Halebid

Kanchipuram

Sravanabelagola

Chennai (Madras)

Mysore

Mahabalipuram

Gangaikondacholapuram

Periyar

Trichy

Darasuram

Cochin

Tanjore

Madurai

Kovalam

N

W

E

S

(Above) Camel driver watches sunset over the desert plains of western Rajasthan (Previous pages) Vivid colours decorate the roof of the Hemis monastery in Ladakh
(Page before previous pages) Diya or an oil lamp floating in the holy waters of the Ganges
(Following page) Multi coloured flags stand in contrast with barren landscape of Ladakh, which falls in the rain shadow area of the Himalayas.
The flags have Buddhist prayer written on them and the breeze carries the prayers to heaven (Pages 10-11) Women in colourful sarees take a holy dip in the river Yamuna
with Taj Mahal in the background. Hindus consider the river holy as it flows into the Ganges in the city of Allahabad
(Pages 12-13) Lush green landscape of Periyar forest in south India is home to wide variety of wild animals which can be seen on the shores of the lake
(Pages 14-15) Kutch in Gujarat forms the western most frontier of India. Its inhabitants live in harsh dry climate.
In contrast to their habitat they adorn themselves in colourful dresses that are embroidered locally

India is one of the oldest civilizations in the world, a vast sub-continent of tremendous complexity, contradictions and great natural beauty. The mainland comprises of four distinct regions, namely the mountain zone or the Himalayan range, the plains of Ganges and the Indus, the desert region of Rajasthan in the west. The fourth is the southern peninsula. It is like an inverted triangle with western and eastern ghats facing the Arabian sea and the Bay of Bengal and the Deccan plateau in the middle. Offshore lie the Andaman and Nicobar islands in the Bay of Bengal extending all the way down to the Indian Ocean. The Union Territory of Lakshadweep in Arabian Sea constitutes twenty-seven islands, out of which only ten are inhabited.

India is home to one of the greatest civilizations and the birthplace of two major religions, Hinduism and Buddhism. Besides, every other religion is represented here: Islam, Christianity, Jainism, Sikhism, Zorastrianism and Judaism. Because India is essentially a religious society, temples. mosques, churches and gurudwaras are virtually littered across the country. Some of these places of worship are also architectural wonders that draw thousands of tourists every year. Today, India is one of the most democratic secular countries of the world.

Millions of years ago, India, Australia and Africa were one land mass. Due to shifting of continental plates, India separated from the two and pushed itself into the continent of Asia. Hence India is called the sub-continent. This pushing of the continental plates also gave rise to the mighty Himalayas, the temple of snow, where as many as ninety-five peaks are more than seven thousand five hundred meters high. The Indian sub-continent is still pushing into the Asian continent. For this reason the height of the mountain peaks in the Himalayas is still increasing and the Indian sub-continent time and again experiences devastating earthquakes.

The original inhabitants of India were very similar to the aborigines of Australia. Some of these tribes, like the Todas of Nilgiri mountains in the south of India, can still be seen. The first evidence of urbanization in the sub-continent is found in the Indus valley in present day Pakistan.

INDUS VALLEY CIVILIZATION

In the northwestern part of Indian sub-continent a highly developed civilization known as the Indus Valley Civilization flourished on the banks of the river Indus in the third millennium B.C. It was home to the largest of the four ancient river valley civilizations of Egypt, Mesopotamia, India and China. Out of these four, the Indian civilization perhaps is the only one that has survived intact. The Indus Valley civilization was the first major urban site in the history of the Indian sub-continent. It revealed the transition of a pastoral to a settled agrarian society. Many Indologists also refer to it as Harappan Culture.

The earliest city to be discovered in the region was Mohenjodaro followed by Harappa, now in Sindh region of Pakistan. At its peak, the Indus Valley Civilization stretched across the whole of Sindh, Baluchistan, Punjab, Haryana, Rajasthan, Kathiawar and Gujarat. Its cities were far more advanced than their counterparts in Egypt, Mesopotamia or elsewhere in western Asia. As in most other contemporary civilizations, agriculture was the backbone of the Indus economy. The strong Indian bull, with its natural hump, helped to get more land under cultivation. Wooden ploughs had been in use since early-Harappan times (3000-2300 B.C.) as evidenced by furrow marks found during the excavations at Kalibangan. As the agricultural base expanded, trading started which gave birth to many towns, mainly along the region of Doab, the land between two tributaries of the river Indus.

The cities were well planned and great care was taken to look after them properly. The streets ran straight and at right angles to each other. They were wide with houses built of burnt bricks on both sides. There were drains alongside the roads. People were prosperous and had leisure for both amusement and contemplation.

The climate of the north- western region of India was not as arid as it is now. In those days Sindh and Rajasthan were covered with thick forests, which provided timber for building boats and brick- kilns. The land was fertile and barley and wheat were the main food crops. Perhaps the most important achievement was the cultivation of cotton. There is also evidence of the domestication of cats, dogs, goats, sheep and perhaps the elephant.

The Indus people made extensive use of bronze, copper and gold. However, iron was discovered later in 800 B.C. The people were very artistic. Evidence can be found in the pottery, stone sculpture and seal-making. The pottery was made of well-levigated and well-fired clay, painted in black pigment.

The Harappans worshipped natural elements such as the tree, humped bull and the mother goddess. They believed in life after death because their graves contained household pottery, ornaments and mirrors, which may

(Previous pages) Anjanta caves are world renowned for their frescoes. The interiors of these fifth century temples and monasteries are beautifully decorated with narrative paintings on the life of earlier Buddhas known as the Boddhisattvas

have belonged to the dead person and which he took along for his use in his after-life.

Unlike their counterparts in the rest of the world, who were ruled by kings, the Indus people were managed by a group of merchants. They had commercial links with the people in Afghanistan, Persia, Egypt, Mesopotamia and the Sumer. Trade was in the form of barter. There was a cleverly organized system of weights and measures in various shapes and very accurately graded. The script was pictographic which unfortunately has not been deciphered as yet.

There is a striking contrast between the civilizations of the west and the Indus Valley in the way it was governed. In Egypt and Sumer much money and thought were lavished in building magnificent temples, palaces and tombs for kings. The common people however were confined to small dwellings of mud. In the Indus Valley the picture is reversed. The finest structures were erected for the convenience of the citizens. This is evident from the remains of the Great Bath at Mohenjodaro and the granaries.

The Indus Valley Civilization lasted for about a thousand years and after 2000 B.C. slowly declined and disappeared. Some historians ascribe this to the decreasing fertility of the soil on account of the increasing salinity caused by the expansion of the neighbouring desert. Others attribute this to some kind of depression in the land which caused floods. Still others believe that the Aryan invasion destroyed it. Although there are various theories about the end of the Indus Valley Civilization, there is no definite answer as to how or why it came to an end.

THE VEDIC AGE

Until the discovery of Mohenjodaro and Harappa, it was believed that Indian history and civilization began with the coming of the Aryans. The Indo-European tribes called the Indo-Aryans migrated to the area called Sapta-Sindhu or the land of seven rivers around 1500 B.C. (There is no archaeological evidence of the migration of the Aryans; many believe they were the wandering tribes of aborigines.) . The Aryans prepared the first and oldest collection of

mystical hymns known as the Rig Veda, which is the only source of information on early Vedic life. Yajur, Sama and Atharva Vedas followed the Rig Veda. Archaeological evidence is greatly enhanced when used in association with other historical sources. Since the earlier Indus inscriptions are yet to be fully deciphered, the Vedas assume considerable significance for scholars. It was handed down orally from generation to generation and gives an early glimpse of religion, agriculture and society in the Punjab and North India.

The Aryans came as pastoral nomads and kept large herds of cattle. The tribal nature of their society was transformed after they reached the Indo-Gangetic plain. The Aryans made the fertile region between the two rivers Ganges and Jamuna called Doab their home and gradually gave up the nomadic way of life and took to settled agriculture. With permanency, Aryan societies soon evolved stable forms of local government and administration. This led to a person being elected from the people with the help of the Samiti and Sabha.

Samiti were assemblies where the whole tribe was present and everyone was free to voice their opinion. The Sabha consisted of the village elders and appears to have been a smaller assembly of selected people. The selected head was called Raja or King. He had the responsibility to administer, defend the tribe and collect agricultural revenue. Brahmins or the priests were his advisors. They recited the Vedas and interpreted them for the rest of the tribe. Although the Raja had limited powers, they were kept in check by the elders. The Sabha and Samiti were the guardians of society and even empowered to overthrow the Raja if the style of governance did not meet with their approval.

The Aryans believed in nature worship. Indra was the god of rain, storm and war; Surya was the sun-god; Agni was the fire-god; and Usha was the goddess of dawn. All ceremonies were centreed around the fire god, Agni, because he was considered a purifier. Sacrifices and chanting of the Vedic hymns, that were believed to have magical powers, formed the most important part of religious worship. Basically, these ceremonies were preformed to appease the elements.

The other important texts to follow the Vedas were the Brahmanas. These gave detailed explanations of the various rituals and ceremonies. Later, the epics of Ramayana and Mahabharata became important religious texts. Puranas or the old texts give the descriptions of the rulers and their origin.

But not all people were satisfied with the religion of elaborate rituals and sacrifices. They questioned the role of the priest as the messenger between God and man. The ideas of these philosophers were recorded in texts called the Upanishads, which are part of the Vedas. Upanishad scholars raised the question of Brahman — the Supreme Being

A Mughal flower medallion from the tomb of Itmad-ud-Daulah

from which everything emanates and eventually dissipates into. Karma, or the sum total of acts done in one stage of person's existence, which determine his destiny in next life, was also perpetuated during the Vedic period.

The Doab region soon became an established home for the Aryans and was called Aryavrata. The war that established the supremacy in the region was fought between two Brahmin priests, Vishwamitra and Vashistha. Vashistha had the support of the warring clan of Bharathas who eventually established their supremacy in the region. They called their kingdom Bharatvarsha, which is still the name of India in Hindi.

As trade grew in the villages along the Ganges, the people within each society came to be recognized by their principal occupation. This was the beginning of caste system in India. Society was divided into different jatis or castes. The Brahmins or priests were responsible for teaching of the Vedas and setting an example of rightful living. Kshatriyas or warriors were responsible for maintaining law and order and provide protection against invaders. The Vaishyas were the merchants, artisans and peasants. And finally the Shudras were the outcastes that were assigned menial tasks and lived on the outskirts of the villages.

Initially the caste divisions were very fluid. People could easily change their caste according to the profession they chose to pursue, until an increasingly rigid social code decreed that birth and heredity alone would determine one's caste.

As the Aryan civilization grew, the tribes expanded eastwards along the Gangetic plain. Gradually sixteen large territorial states or Mahajanpadas were formed. Of these Magadha, Kosala, Vatsa and Avanti were most powerful. They fought among themselves for political pre-eminence for about hundred years. Magadha under the leadership of Bimbisara (542 - 493 B.C.) and Ajatshatru (493 – 461 B.C.) emerged victorious. The victory of Magadha firmly established the monarchical system in the Ganges plain. Ajatshatru was succeeded by Udayan (460 - 444 B.C.). His reign saw the establishment of a new capital at Patliputra (modern day Patna). The architecture of the Magadhan Empire is the first of which we have any contemporary record.

The Shishunaga dynasty, which followed in 413 B.C., lasted barely half a century and gave way to the Nanda dynasty. In the fourth century Magadha was ruled by the Nanda kings and was the most powerful kingdom in the north. The Nandas had collected a vast amount of wealth in taxes and kept a huge standing army, but their inefficiency led to their overthrow by Chandragupta Maurya who conspired with Chanakya, the minister of the Nandas to defeat them.

THE GREEK INVASIONS

In the 326 B.C. Alexander the Great marched with his army to northwest India. He was on a winning roll. Greece, Egypt and the mighty Persian Empire had all been defeated by his military genius. After conquering Bactria he marched on to through Hindu Kush mountains. He annexed Taxila and entered further into the plains of Punjab. At the banks of the river Beas, a tributary of Indus he was challenged by King Porus. Alexander easily outwitted the strong opposition. He asked the captured king what treatment he should be given. "Same as one king expects of another king," replied Porus. Alexander was so impressed by the reply that he gave back the kingdom to Porus. Alexander was known to be extremely generous but could be viciously cruel too.

Finally in July, his homesick army refused to cross into the hot plains of northern India. They had traversed eleven thousand miles in the last seven years.

Many of his generals stayed back and left a mark on the art and culture of India forever. Alexander's influence brought to bear upon Indian art, architecture and philosophy a Grecian style, which was further re-inforced by King Meander (155 – 130 B.C.), who expanded the Indo-Greek Kingdom of Bactria to include part of the Punjab. The Indo-Greeks were the first to issue gold coins with the name, title and portrait of the ruler embossed on the coins. This was an era symbol-ized by progress and upheavals in kingdoms and cultural fusions. All this radically altered the very fabric of social life in India and brought about dramatic changes in Indian art.

For almost 1000 years, Taxila (in modern day Pakistan) remained an important religious, commercial and artistic centre. During the first century, the Kushan Empire spanned from Peshawar, in the extreme northwest, to Benaras in the east, with centres also at Gandhara and Mathura. The Greeks heavily influenced the Buddhist art of this period. It was in the reign of the Kushan king Kanishka that the first human image of Buddha was carved out. Much of this art form around Peshawar and the Swat Valley in Pakistan's northern border can be seen today in museums at Mathura and New Delhi.

MAURYAN EMPIRE (321 – 185 B.C.)

Although Alexander's invasion left an indelible influence on Indian art and culture, its influence was confined to north western India. For the rest, the Nandas were firmly in control. They were defeated by Chandragupt Maurya who united the whole of northern India under his able administration. We have a fairly detailed description of the glories of the Mauryan Empire from Megasthenes, the Greek ambassador in the court of Chandragupta in the capital city of Patliputra. Megasthenes wrote his observations in a book called Indica, describing the splendors of the capital city Patliputra and the empire as whole. After Alexander's death, Seleucus, the governor of the Greek Empire surrendered the Hindu Kush area to Chandragupta. This marked the first step in the expansion and consolidation of the Mauryan Empire. Megasthenes tells us that a thousand-mile highway connected Patliputra to Peshawar.

Provinces were ruled by governors and viceroys. The emperor himself was advised by the council of ministers. An extensive irrigation system was regulated through a network of canals and the farmers were well respected. Even at the time of war, they worked in their fields. The real genius behind the able administration of the state was Kautilya, the chief administrator of Chandragupta. He wrote Arthasastra, a book that lays down the economic, political and legal responsibilities of the state.

Trade flourished, agriculture was regulated, and weights and measures were standardized. It was at this time that money replaced barter and first came into use. Taxation, sanitation and famine relief became the concerns of the State. It is said that towards the end of his rule Chandragupta was converted to Jainism. His son and successor Bindusara (298 – 273 B.C.) extended the kingdom further as far as Mysore in the south. It was under his son Ashoka that the Mauryan Empire reached the peak of its glory.

Ashoka (273 - 232 B.C.) won over Kalinga in eastern India in 265 B.C. and for the first time the whole of the sub-continent, except the extreme south, was under imperial control. It is said that the conquest of Kalinga resulted in 100,000 dead and 150,000 prisoners, while thousands died of pestilence and hunger. Stricken by remorse Ashoka embraced Buddhism.

Ashoka propagated Buddhism in the kingdoms of the Cholas and the Pandyas in south India and in five Greek states of the northwest. He sent his brother Mahendra with a sapling of Bodhi tree (under which Buddha had attained enlightenment), which was planted at Anuradhapura in central Ceylon. He also sent missionaries to Swarnbhumi (Burma) and also parts of South East Asia. He was the first ruler to maintain direct contact with his people through various edicts, which were composed in Prakrit and written in Brahmi script. They were engraved on rocks, pillars and caves propagating his ideas on religion and the relationship between the government and the people. These edicts are in the form of forty four royal orders, which aim at moulding the general behavior of the people. It is because of these rock edicts that Ashoka's teachings are still alive. Stone masonry was introduced on a wide scale. The emblem of the Indian Republic has been adopted from the four-lions capital of Ashoka's pillar at Sarnath near Varanasi.

The Mauryan administration was highly centralized. The state maintained a huge standing army. Taxes were collected from various sources. The State brought new lands under cultivation and developed irrigation facilities. It was under the Mauryans that the royal highway connecting Taxila and Patliputra was constructed – a road that survives to date as the Grand Trunk Road. Mauryan artisans had started the practice of hewing out caves from rocks for the monks to live in. The earliest examples are the Barabar hill caves near Gaya. Stupas were built throughout the empire to enshrine the relics of Buddha. Of these the most famous one is at Sanchi, in central India. It is the oldest surviving architectural heritage of India.

The Mauryan Empire lasted a little over a century and broke up fifty years after the death of Ashoka. It was the weak successors of Ashoka that brought about its dismemberment. Gradually the various princes of the empire began to break away and set up independent kingdoms. Finally in 185 B.C., Pushyamitra Shunga, an ambitious general of the armed forces, assassinated the Mauryan king Brihadratha. He started the Shunga dynasty in Magadha. The Mauryan Empire, which lasted for about two hundred years, was a glorious chapter in Indian history.

After the breakup of the Mauryan Empire, a number of foreign powers came to India in waves and contributed to its culture. The main invaders were the Bactrian Greeks ruled by Demetrius II (180 -165 B.C.) and Menander (155 -130 B.C.). The Satavahanas, the Shakas and the Kushans ruled in various parts of the subcontinent from first century before Christ to third century after. Kanishka was the most celebrated ruler of this period. What was to follow is termed as the Classical Age dominated by the Gupta dynasty.

The Guptas (300 - 700 A.D.)

In the fourth century A.D., a new dynasty arose in the Ganga valley, which established a large kingdom over the greater part of northern and central India. This was the Gupta dynasty that ushered in the classical age of Indian history. Lasting for over four centuries the Gupta era continued to see some of the great achievements of Indian culture, which had begun in the earlier period. Not only were they powerful monarchs, they were also patrons of learning and encouraged poets, writers, scientists and artisans, all of whom contributed to Indian culture.

The origin of the Guptas is shrouded in mystery. Probably they were a family of wealthy landowners who gradually gained political control in the region of Magadha. The founder of the Gupta dynasty, Chandragupta I ascended the throne in about 320 A.D. The kingdom was enlarged

An Indus Valley Civilization seal dating back to 2500 B.C. showing the humped bull

by his son, Samudragupta, who fought against a number of kings and annexed territories in the northern part of the sub-continent. However, his direct political control was only over the Ganges Valley, as compared to the Mauryan Empire, which extended to south India. It was during the reign of Samudragupta's successor, Chandragupta II (also known as Vikramaditya), that the Gupta ascendancy reached its peak. They consolidated their empire by making matrimonial alliances with the neighbouring kingdoms of Licchavis and also with Vatakas in the south.

During the reign of the Guptas the classical arts flourished. Shakuntala, the famous play written by Kalidas and Kamasutra, the Indian treatise on love making by Vatsayana, exemplify the literary craftsmanship of this period. The Panchatantra, a collection of fables was another popular work. Many outstanding contributions to metallurgy, mathematics and the sciences, originated during this time. An iron pillar erected in Delhi inscribed with the name of Chandragupta II (373 - 414) stands under open skies without a trace of rust. It is a fine example of the advanced metallurgical practices of the day. The astronomer Aryabhatta conceived the theory that the earth orbited around the sun. He also calculated Pi as 3.1416 and is attributed as the inventor of the numeral zero. Later the Indian numerals were carried to the west by the Arab merchants and hence called the Arabic numerals.

Nagara and Dravida styles of temple architecture, the earliest surviving temples in India- originate from this period. The cave paintings of Ajanta displayed highly developed narrative and religious themes. The Shastra (texts) for the Vastu (architecture), Shilpa (sculpture) and Chitra (painting) were laid down during this glorious classical era, which continue to be referred to in modern times. Bhakti movement took firm hold in the ritual worship. Six schools of Hindu philosophy were founded at this time. These were Nyaya (analysis), Vaisheshika (particular characterstics), Sankhya (enumeration), Yoga (application), Mimamsa (inquiry), and Vedanta (end of Vedas), whose final purpose was the union of individual and Absolute Soul after death.

The Guptas declined as a result of the devastation caused by the waves of the Hun invaders. The Huns were part of Ephthalites or white Huns who originated from the Oxus Valley in the Hindu Kush mountains. On the footsteps of Huns followed more central Asian tribes who are the forefathers of many of the Rajput clans.

From the decline of the Guptas until the rise of Harshavardhan in the early seventh century, the political scene is confused and there are sketchy records to illuminate it. In this period, it was in the southern kingdoms that the Indian civilization showed its greatest vitality.

Harshavardhan (606 - 647)

The second half of the seventh century witnessed the empire building efforts of Harshavardhan who belonged to the Pushabhukti family. He ruled northern India including Punjab, eastern Rajasthan and the Ganga valley as far as Assam, with capitals at Thaneshwar, and later Kanauj. His reign is well documented in Bana's(his court poet) 'Harshacharita', an account of his rise to power, and in the travel accounts of the Chinese pilgrim, Hieun Tsang.

In his travelogue the Chinese pilgrim has recorded the existence of a rigid caste system that increasingly became more discriminatory. But he was particularly impressed by the spread of Buddhism and Nalanda University in Bihar, which had 4,000 students enrolled. The university library was stocked with all the major texts on Buddhist philosophy and, when the Turks burned down this mine of knowledge in the twelfth century, it is said that the manuscripts took three months to burn.

Harshavardhan governed his empire on the same lines as the Guptas. His empire included distant territories of feudal kings who paid him revenue and sent soldiers in time of war. They accepted his sovereignty but remained rulers of their own kingdoms.

Harshavardhan's empire collapsed soon after his death. Without an heir, the kingdom rapidly disintegrated into small states. The succeeding period is obscure and poorly documented, but it marks the culmination of a process which had begun with the invasion of the Huns in the last years of the Gupta Empire.

Southern Kingdoms (500 - 900)

Meanwhile the kingdoms in the Deccan and the south India became very powerful. The kingdoms that dominated were those of the Chalukyas, Pallavas and Pandyas. The Chalukyas built great capitals and temples at Badami, Aihole and Pattadakal in Karnatka in the south. The Pallavas ruled in the southeast with their capital at Kanchipuram, while along the Western Ghats and the Deccan, the Rashtrakutas governed near Bombay and Ellora.

The south Indian rulers were great patrons of temple architecture, as is evident from the magnificent temples of Thanjavur, Kanchipuram and Gangaikondacholapuram in south India. Under their patronage, bronze sculpture also flourished. The Nataraja, or the dancing figure of Shiva, is considered a masterpiece of Chola art.

As a result of northern domination of Indian culture, the south has been largely overshadowed. This is unfortunate since the fields of art, architecture and philosophy that emerged from the south have a distinct influence and flavour.

The Rajputs (700 — 1200)

The great kingdoms of Rajputana (present day Rajasthan) were ruled by princely clans called Rajputs, literally 'sons of kings', who controlled the northwestern boundaries for over thousand years. The Rajputs were fiercely independent and they would rather die in a battle than be held in captivity. The Rajput women were renowned for their pride and preferred to throw themselves into funeral pyres instead of getting captured by the enemy. Rani Padmini, the wife of a Sisodian Chief, first carried out this act of 'Jauhar', or collective sacrifice in Chittor.

There are various theories about the historical origin of the Rajputs. Some claim to be descendents of the Gurjara Pratiharas, the earliest of Rajput dynasties, which later went on to hold the balance of power throughout Rajasthan. There is also evidence to suggest that some Rajput clans can trace their emergence to the arrival of foreign invaders from Central Asia, who may have settled and consequently been assimilated into the region.

While questions about their actual origin remain unanswered, the Rajputs seem to have developed a complex mythological genealogy. The Suryavanshi clans claim descent from the Sun; the Chadravanshis from the Moon; and a third branch called the Agnikula, or Fire Born. These Rajputs were manifested from the flames of a sacrificial pyre at Mt. Abu. Thirtysix clans of Rajputs have emerged from these three races.

The Rajputs have a proud history. Being a frontier state, which lay on the trade route of the west, Rajasthan bore the brunt of many foreign invasions. First came the Arab invaders followed by the Afghans. The Rajput princes combined their forces and tried to put up a front against Mahmud of Ghazni in 1001, and Muhammad Ghori towards the end of the twelfth century, but failed in their attempt. The most famous Rajput ruler of this time was Prithvi Raj Chuhan. He ruled the Tomar kingdom from Quila Rai Pithora in Delhi. He wooed the daughter of the enemy king of Kanauj. Their elopement is immortalised by the epic poem Prithvirajaraso of Chand Bardai. He repulsed the attack of the first wave of the Muslim invaders in the battle of Train in the year 1191 although in the following year he was killed by Muhammad Ghori.

The Arab and the Turks were the new dominant force in North India. The Arabs captured Sindh in 713. Later the invasions of the Turks came at regular intervals. The temple towns of Kanauj and Somnathpur, fabled for their gold and riches, were repeatedly looted. The local kings were divided by their petty differences to form any formidable opposition to the maundering invaders. In the invasion of 1206 Mahummad Ghori left behind one of his slaves to govern Delhi and its neighborhood. On the death of Mahummad Ghori in Afganistan the slave general crowned himself as the first Sultan of Delhi.

THE COMING OF THE MUSLIMS

The Delhi Sultanate (1206 - 1526)

Qutab-ud-din Aibak formed a new state with Delhi as its capital and Islam as its official religion. Later Aibak's lieutenant Iltutmish seized power from him and made Delhi his capital.

Turkish slaves or Mamluks who were the military leaders, governors and officers in court dominated the Delhi Sultanate. This is the reason why the term Slave Dynasty or Slave Sultanate is applied. However, this is misleading as only two sultans, Iltutmish and Balban were slaves. The Mamluks were threatened by the growing numbers of immigrants including nobles, bureaucrats and soldiers who sought asylum in India after the Mongols devastated Central Asia.

In 1290 the Khaljis, who were immigrants of Turkish stock, succeeded Balban. In spite of the Khalji accession to power the slaves continued to play an influential role in the Delhi Sultanate. The newly- born Sultanate was weakened by internal dissensions and factionalism between the Mamluks and the non-Mamluks. Mention must be made of Raziyyia, Iltutmish's daughter who was the first woman sovereign in the Islamic world. It was not until the victory of Balban in 1265 . that the Sultanate obtained some degree of stability.

In the first half of the thirteenth century the threat of the Mongols was growing in the northwest and resulted in the sacking of Lahore. Thereafter the Mongol invasions were a common occurrence. The advent of the Khalji dynasty came around the same time as the Mongol occupation of Afghanistan. A direct result of this was the building up of the Mongol pressure on India.

The Sultanate maintained large armies for defense against the formidable Mongol threat. The resources to maintain huge armies came from the expeditions against the Hindu states. However, the Sultanate overstretched its resources and bought on its own collapse.

The Tughluq dynasty succeeded the Khaljis in 1320 Ghias-ud-Din Tughluq's son Muhammad was probably the most well-known ruler of the dynasty. He made the more centrally located Daulatabad his capital and started the Muslim colonization of Deccan. He took the offensive against Mongols and planned an expedition into Afghanistan.

Although the Delhi Sultanate had come to occupy a vast territory, they ruled over a society in which they were all a minority. As a result the Tughluq reign saw a number of revolts by Hindu provinces that finally led to its disintegration.

The Saiyyads and then the Lodis succeeded the

Tughluqs. The end of the Lodi era saw the advent of the Mughal power in India. At the battle of Panipat in 1526, Babur, a descendent of Timur and Genghis Khan, defeated and killed the last Lodi ruler, Ibrahim Lodi. This was the beginning of a new chapter in the history of India as Zahir-ud-Din Muhammad Babur went on to become the first Emperor of the Mughal dynasty in India.

THE MUGHAL EMPIRE, (1526 - 1707)
Babur (1526- 1530)

Babur founded the Mughal Empire in India that finally stretched from its northern boundaries to the Deccan. It was in Kabul, where Babur ruled, that he saw the caravans loaded with silver, gold, silks, ivory and spices coming from India. This aroused his curiosity about India's fabulous riches. He saw an opportunity in the power struggles among the Turkish rulers of north India that led to a vacuum in power.

He took advantage of this situation and defeated the army of the Turkish ruler, Ibrahim Lodhi at Panipat in north India in 1526. Soon after, he was crowned the Emperor of Hindustan. Although Babur had defeated the Lodhis, he faced imminent danger from the fierce Rajput king, Rana Sanga of Mewar. The king's bravery was legendary. However, Babur managed to crush the Rajput army and the battle of Khanua in 1527 established Mughal supremacy in India.

As Emperor of Hindustan, Babur could now pursue his passion for reading literature and composing poetry. His work, the 'Babur Nama', initiated the royal tradition of writing auto- biographies among his successors.

Babur was in possession of the famous Kohinoor (mountain of light) diamond. Legend has it that if sold it could feed the whole world for two and a half days. The diamond was later cut into three pieces and currently adorns the British crown.

Babur did not enjoy the fruits of his victory for very long. He died four years after his Indian conquest, and was buried in Kabul, according to his last wishes.

Humayun (1530 - 1556)

Humayun, Babur's son, inherited a vast though unstable empire, which covered much of northern India and was constantly under threat by the Rajputs and Afghans. His first task therefore was to suppress rebellions in the newly formed empire, and to consolidate it.

However he failed to do so and was forced to flee to Persia in 1540 after his defeat by Sher Shah Suri, who suc- ceeded him. The Afghan ruler has the unique status of being the only non - Mughal who dared to lead the Mughal Empire.

Humayun returned to India in 1555 after an accident brought an end to Sher Shah's life. He was able to rule for only six months before falling to his death from a staircase in Purana Qila or the Old Fort in Delhi. A historian who said, 'Humayun tumbled through life and tumbled out of it', aptly summed up the life of this ineffectual ruler.

Humayun's widow built an exquisite tomb in his memory in Delhi. This started the charbagh (four gardens) tomb tradition in Mughal architecture that was to culminate eighty years later in the building of the Taj Mahal.

Akbar, (1556- 1605)

Akbar was, in a sense, the true founder of the Mughal Empire. He was only fourteen when news of his father's death reached him. The new Emperor, despite his young age, man- aged to consolidate the gains of his grandfather, Babur.

Akbar's prime achievement was the creation of an administrative framework, which sustained his Empire for about one hundred and fifty years. He evolved a new pattern of king-noble relationship, which suited the needs of a federal state. He realized that in order to strengthen his sprawling empire, which covered the north and the far- flung areas in south India, he needed the support of local chieftains. Instead of antagonizing them and in order to strike a balance in the ruling class he promoted Persians, Indian Muslims and Rajputs to Imperial service. He even married several Hindu princesses and observed important Hindu festivals like Holi and Diwali.

In spite of being illiterate, Akbar was an ardent patron of the arts. Under his patronage several Indian religious texts were translated into Persian, and Islamic works translated into Sanskrit.

Akbar was the greatest of Mughal rulers and was the first truly secular leader of India. He recognized the impor- tance of harmony between communities for the strength and survival of a nation and managed to hold a vast empire together by inspiring respect for all religions. Akbar built the city of Fatehpur Sikri, near Agra, and dedicated it to the Sufi saint, Sheikh Salim Chisti. Akbar passed away in 1605. Sikandra, eight kilome- ters from Agra was to be his final resting place.

Jehangir (1605- 1628)

The reign of Jehangir was noted for its political stability. Instead of strengthening the vast Empire he inherited from his illustrious father, he preferred to lead a degenerate life and surrounded himself with wine and women.

Jehangir's most significant political achievement was the ending of the conflict between the Mughals and the King of Mewar. But typically for the Mughals, his son Khusrau rebelled against him and Jehangir had him blinded and consigned to jail.

Such harsh measures discouraged any future rebel- lions. Jehangir's other son, prince Khurram proved successful in his campaigns in the Deccan and the Marwar. This earned him the title of Shah Jahan, 'ruler of the world'.

During Jehangir's rule nepotism and political intrigue

became widespread and his wife Nur Jahan practically dealt with all the affairs of the kingdom. Such was her influence over political matters that her father was called Itidmaud Dhaula, the pillar of the state and brother too held powerful position in the court of emperor Jehangir. With Jehangir's death in 1627, Shah Jahan took over the kingdom but against powerful opposition from within the family.

Shah Jahan, (1628 – 1658)

Shah Jahan's reign is best remembered for his great contributions to architecture that made it famous throughout the world. He built the magnificent Taj Mahal, one of the Seven Wonders of the World, as a memorial for his favourite queen, Mumtaz Mahal. It took twenty-two years to be completed and twenty thousand workers, artisans and master craftsmen worked on the site. The Taj Mahal is an architectural marvel and represents the epitome of Mughal architecture. Shah Jahan also built the Red Fort and the Jama Masjid in his new capital called Shahjahanbad in Delhi. His love for monuments earned him the title of the 'great builder' and all these structures were built under his personal supervision.

Shah Jahan's extravagant tastes included his love for jewels and led him to create the spectacular Peacock Throne. Probably the most expensive throne ever commissioned, it was studded with diamonds, rubies and pearls and weighed a ton in pure gold. However all these extravagances drained the royal treasury and indirectly created a bitter power struggle among his children. Towards the end of his reign the treasury was almost empty and the amount of crown land vastly reduced.

Eventually, Aurangzeb, Shah Jahan's youngest son, led a rebellion against his father and had his brothers killed in order to succeed the throne. In 1666 Shah Jahan died in captivity in Agra Fort and was succeeded by Aurangzeb.

Aurangzeb (1658 - 1707)

Unlike his ancestors who believed in religious tolerance, Aurangzeb was a fundamentalist. He ruled his empire on the basis of Shariyat, the orthodox Muslim religious law. He reimposed the Jizyah [religious] tax on non- Muslims, stopped the construction of new temples and destroyed and desecrated existing ones such as the Somnath, Vishwanath and Keshavrai temples. Aurangzeb's religious fundamentalism and unfair policies alienated the Hindus and led him to unnecessary confrontations with powerful Hindus like the Marathas under the formidable Shivaji.

Aurangzeb's death in 1707 was the final nail in the coffin and was followed by a series of bloody battles of succession. This was the beginning of the disintegration of the Mughal Empire and once again India was too weak and divided to resist foreign aggression. First among the invaders was Nadir Shah of Persia who plundered Delhi in 1739. He looted the city for two months, stripping the palaces of their gold and silver.

Among many precious possessions he carried away was also the Peacock Throne.

By the second half of the eighteenth century, the British and Europeans had begun to make inroads into India and started absorbing small kingdoms into the areas they administered. Finally the deeply fragmented Mughal Empire could offer little resistance to the conquering armies and fell an easy prey to the British.

THE BRITISH IN INDIA

The discovery of the sea route by the Portuguese explorer, Vasco da Gama in 1498 brought India to the attention of European maritime powers. The discovery eliminated Arabs who hitherto dominated Indian trade. Their place was now taken by European powers represented by Portugese, Dutch, French and later by the British. For a while, Britain bought Indian goods from the Dutch but as the cost of imports increased, it was inevitable that Britain started trading directly.

Surat in Gujarat was the first place where the British formed their trading posts after the Mughals granted them trading rights.

From 1600 - 1757 the role of the European East India Companies, set up by the English, French, Dutch and Portuguese, was that of a trading corporation. These companies bought Indian goods, mainly cotton, spices, silk, muslin, ivory and precious stones. In return India got gold bullions which benefited India as it ensured a steady income of gold. It increased the export of Indian manufacturers and even encouraged production. India was the sole beneficiary and Indian rulers tolerated, even encouraged, the establishment of East India Company factories in their kingdoms.

Gradually these European companies became competitive over their respective spheres of influence and started absorbing small kingdoms into the areas they administered. The British and the French were already involved in power struggles in Europe which were now extended to India. The British emerged victorious after they were able to crush the weakening Mughal Empire and successfully ruled India for the next two hundred years.

The battle of Plassey in 1757 in eastern India established the British stronghold in Bengal. The British led by Robert Clive also asserted their authority over the French in the south. The imperial forces of the Mughal tried in vain to

Typical Indian dagger Katar was the preferred weapon of the Rajput kings

stop the growing threat of the British. The Mughal forces were eventually defeated in the battle of Buxar in 1764. These two victories proved crucial in gaining economic control over the people of Bengal and north India.

From this time onwards trade relations between India and Europe underwent a change. The nature of the trade was the same but instead of the Indians benefiting, the British did. Soon after the British got Diwani (revenue administration) of Bengal, Bihar and Orrisa. They then started paying for the Indian goods out of the revenue instead of the gold bullion. As a result there was no influx of money into the economy.

Around this period the British introduced the Permanent Settlement. This entitled them to a substantial portion of the state revenue and set up a feudal system of aristocracy, with the result that the peasants became poorer as the landlords harassed them for greater output to meet the demands of the British. Subsequently the British gained control over other territories and their economic supremacy translated itself to political supremacy. By 1848 with the annexation of Punjab the East India Company was the new ruler of India.

The people protested against the growing British dominance but these uprisings were few and far between. The Sepoy Mutiny in 1857 was based on the rumour that the cartridges supplied were greased with cow and pig fat which was a taboo with Hindus and Muslims. This enraged the Hindu and Muslim sentiments of the Sepoys who were ninety percent of the company forces. This was the first organized revolt of some significance. However it proved to be a failure, as it lacked nationwide support. Bahadur Shah Zafar, the powerless Mughal ruler, was reluctantly made the leader of the uprising. In 1857 British marched inside the Red Fort of Delhi, the seat of the Mughal Empire and exiled the old emperor to Burma.

The revolt of 1857 brought about a permanent change in the nature of the British rule. The British took drastic measures to safeguard their Imperial authority and check the rising tide of rebellion. An Act of Parliament in 1858 abolished the East India Company and the British Crown now assumed direct control over India. The viceroy served as the chief administrator and the army was reorganized to increase the number of British officials.

The princes who supported the British during the revolt were handsomely awarded and had become loyal supporters of the British so that when the national movement erupted many of the princes actually crushed the rebellions that were within their jurisdiction. The experience of the revolt had convinced the British that the princely states would serve as allies in case the need arose. In return, the British promised never to annex their territories. The Princes became loyal to the British and from now on ceased to play an important part in Indian politics.

The British policy of economic and political exploitation resulted in a huge economic drain and the nation still has to recover from its impact. The roots of huge economic disparity between the people of India were laid during the British rule, and continue to be an important factor hindering the development of the country.

However, there were some benefits. India saw the establishment of railways and telegraph, factories and universities. Indians were allowed to enter the civil services which enabled them to have some control in the administration of the country. Social problems like sati, child marriage, female infanticide and widow remarriage were addressed and reforms introduced. The 'Brahmo Samaj' and the 'Arya Samaj' were part of the social reform movement and played a significant role in raising social consciousness against the evils of society.

With the birth of the educated middle class and the intellectual awakening of the country came the stirrings of nationalism. People realized that local organization was not sufficient and they needed to establish a nationwide organization to redress their grievances against the British Raj. With the result the Indian National Congress was formed in 1885. To begin with the Congress did not aspire for radical political or social changes. Their methods of operation were extremely moderate, expressed mainly through petitions and meetings. However, soon the Congress was divided into two factions – the moderates and the extremists- and the split primarily occurred due to difference in ideology, goals and tactics.

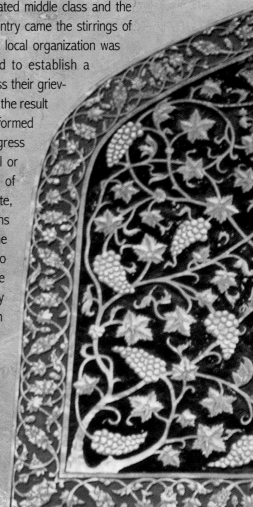

While the moderates believed in peaceful methods and were satisfied with reforms within the confines of British law and government, the extremists agitated for absolute freedom. Furthermore, the achievements of the Congress were greatly undermined not just because of the split but also due to its failure to attract Muslim representatives.

The Muslims were convinced that remaining loyal to the British Raj would best protect their interests. Muslims comprised only one- fifth of the population and they feared subordination by the non-Muslim majority. This resulted in the formation of a separate all India Muslim political organization the Muslim League, in 1906.

However, both the Congress and the League had limited mass appeal as the levers of power were confined to a handful of educated elites. They had to generate far more popular support to prove effective. The mass support for the nationalists came in the early twentieth century. The partition of Bengal by the British in 1905 was seen as an attempt to divide and rule and a series of events that followed offended a wide range of Indian public opinion.

Mohandas Karamchand Gandhi made his entry into the Indian politics in 1915 and his goals of Swaraj or freedom, with the help of Satyagraha, 'truth force', or non-violent resistance to injustice gained ground with the masses. Gandhi launched the non-cooperation movement in 1920 that included boycotting the legislative elections, withdrawal from government law courts and schools and the adoption of Swadeshi, that is, using Indian manufactured goods rather than imports from Britain. Although the movement was a failure, this was the first national level political campaign and it forced the British to review their position in India. The British could derive no economic benefits from India and their ability to manage the Indians had greatly reduced because of important changes in the Indian government and the subsequent growth of the nationalist movement. It became increasingly evident that 'Home Rule' was not sufficient. The persistent demand for freedom culminated in the Quit India Movement of 1942 that forced the British to start conferences with the Indians to grant them freedom.

But complications occurred when the Muslim League demanded the creation of a separate state of Pakistan. They were convinced that partition was the only solution and demanded the inclusion of all the Muslim majority provinces and princely states of India. The British and the Congress dismissed this on practical grounds and hoped that the League would agree on a single state. But by the end of 1946, any evidence of reconciliation was missing and the sub-continent was divided into two independent states of India and Pakistan. Soon after the partition India finally gained Independence on 15th August 1947.

Partition proved to be one of the worst tragedies in the history of independent India. It failed to satisfy the demands of either party and resulted in widespread riots and killings.

The Indian Princely States

At the time of the independence in the year 1947 there were approximately 600 princely states in India. The largest among them was the state of Hyderabad with an area of nearly 80,000 square miles while the smallest was Kathiawar with an area of 1 square mile and the population of a mere 2000 inhabitants. The British saw the Maharajas as enthusiastic supporters of the British raj. This belief was justified as the Maharajas outdid each other in presenting gifts to the Queen Mary, wife of George V, and Empress of India. In 1921 they tried to unite under the banner of 'Chamber of Princes' but the internal differences were so great that they failed to emerge as a political force. After Independence was announced the British gave them three options - to remain independent, be part of India or join the Muslim State of Pakistan. Most of the Maharajas were either cajoled or bullied into ceding their states to the Indian Republic.

However a few princely states remained aloof. The Maharaja of Kashmir was one of the dissenters who decided to remain independent. He was a Hindu monarch who ruled a predominantly Muslim population. The Partition left everyone with a feeling of discontentment. The princes were not invited to the negotiations and Pakistan being a Muslim State, wanted Kashmir to be assimilated into it. They dispatched a small army of Afghans to force the Maharaja into submission. The Hindu king called on Nehru for help and the Indian army was sent to repel the Pakistani attack. The Kashmir issue continues to be the bone of contention between the two neighbouring countries resulting in four wars and an arms race in the region.

Once the Maharajas agreed upon merging with India, they were promised monetary compensation in the form of Privy Purses. The other privileges included diplomatic passports and the right to exemption from paying taxes, they retained their hereditary titles and their car license plates carried their coat of arms.

However Indira Gandhi, who was the Prime Minister, passed a law and amended the constitution according to which all Privy Purses and privileges were withdrawn. On the 28th Dec 1971, fourth President of India V.V. Giri signed the twenty-sixth amendment bill of the constitution, derecognizing the Indian Princes. Privy purses were removed and other privileges withdrawn. Only 22 years previously the princes were coaxed by Sardar Patel, the home minister, to join the Indian Union. The princely families were shocked at how easily a government, who had at the time of Independence asked for their support, could so easily go back on its word. The local government under the urban land ceiling act took a majority of their property away.

The Maharajas who had monetary support were able to convert these structures into the country's finest hotels and museums, but others were not so fortunate.

The erstwhile rulers have no role to play in the Indian administration, though a few represent their subjects in the parliamentary elections. Some are still actively social and can be spotted on the international party circuits on the French Rivera and London. Polo matches are a favourite activity with the princes, a tradition kept alive by the children of the royal families. The processions on the traditional festivals like Dussehra in Mysore and Teej in Jaipur bring back glimpses of a bygone era.

Today, the new Maharajas of Independent India are the democratically elected politicians.

Grapevine detail decorating the entrance of Akbar's tomb at Sikandra near Agra

HINDUISM

To comprehend Indian society, one has to recognise the role religion plays in the lives of the people. Religion permeates every aspect of life in India. The sub-continent has been home to some of the world's major religions: Hinduism, Islam, Christianity, Buddhism, Jainism, Sikhism, Zoroastrianism and Judaism. The influence of these religions over the centuries has resulted in a great deal of religious tolerance and secularism in India, although Hinduism remains the dominant religion of the country.

There is no basic philosophy that describes the beliefs of the majority of India's people. There is no organized Hindu church, no recognized leader of Hinduism, no agreed set of scriptures and no shared doctrines. Unlike other religions that follow precepts set out in religious texts and edicts, Hinduism is more a way of life. It is based on the philosophical traditions that are an amalgamation of the many influences it was subjected to in the past.

To understand Hinduism it is important to appreciate the basic concept of ultimate reality that eventually everything leads to the divine. Three paths have to be traversed in order to be one with the divine- the path of *gyana* [knowledge], the path of *bhakti* (devotion and love) and the path of *karma* (work). These represent the intellectual, emotional and practical aspects of every human being. Yoga is believed to awaken the soul and set it forth on the course of self- realization.

The belief in Karma or one's deeds is central to the Hindu philosophy. All human beings are subject to the cycle of birth and rebirth, depending on the law of karma or deeds in the previous life. The quality of life in the next birth is determined by the deeds performed in this life.

According to the tenets of Hinduism the three principal human goals are material prosperity (*arth*), satisfaction of desires (*kama*), the duties of one's station (*dharma*) and the ultimate goal of all mortals is liberation (*moksha*) from the series of rebirths to which every living being is subject. One of the means of finding release from the cycle of existence is by yoga, which comprises of meditation and exercise and enables the mind and body to recognize one's inner strength.

An ideal Hindu life has four stages of being. The first is studentship or *brahmacharya*; the second is that of a householder or *grihastha*; followed by *vanaprastha* or detachment from worldly goods; and finally *sanyas*, the renunciation of all worldly possessions which is the state of spiritual readiness for liberation or *Moksha*.

Hinduism is also unique among all religions because it is the only religion that believes in caste system. Caste is believed to be determined by one's actions or *Karma* in one's previous life. There are four castes in the Indian society: *Brahmins* or priests, *Kshatriyas* or warriors, *Vaishyas* or the merchants and the *Shudras* or servants.

The principal Hindu texts are the Vedas and the Upanishads. Vedas, meaning knowledge or wisdom, refer to the enormous corpus of Sanskrit texts, which form the authoritative canon of all subsequent forms of orthodox Hinduism. The Vedas are the ancient hymns, which are at the heart of Hindu teachings. They celebrate the oneness of divine principle and man's union with Nature. The Vedas stress on ritualistic worship and sacrifices.

From this evolved the practice of *yajna*, which entails the lighting of a fire before the commencement of a ceremony. In time, these rituals gained stature over the Vedic teachings where performance of rituals alone was considered sufficient to absolve and purify the sinner.

The Upanishads are the seminal works of Hinduism and deal with mystical speculations about a man's life and his place in the universe. According to the Upanishads, the essence of our existence is complete only when it unites with the *Param-atman*, the divine being.

Another important Hindu religious text is the Bhagwad Gita. The epic Mahabharata, which contains the Gita, shows strong links with the Upanishads. The Gita encapsulates the discourse of Lord Krishna, an incarnation of Vishnu, with Arjuna, leader of Pandavas. The essence of the teachings of the Bhagwad Gita is the importance of duty, the immortality of the soul, renunciation of worldly attachments and also the necessity to dedicate the fruit of one's work to the divine.

The Indian religious literature is a veritable storehouse of myths and explains complex philosophical precepts through simple stories, which are easy to comprehend. Many of them are contained in the two great epics of Mahabharata and the Ramayana.

Hinduism is different from other religions in as much as it does not have a single God that the Hindus look to for divine guidance and inspiration. There are myriad gods and goddesses of the Hindu pantheon that epitomize different virtues or forces of nature. The most fundamental to Hinduism is the trinity of Brahma, Vishnu and Mahesh-Creator, Preserver and Destroyer.

India has been a receiver of religions and religious influences from outside from time immemorial. Small Jewish, Christian and Parsi communities have flourished for centuries. However, the greatest impact has been from the Muslims. From a few thousand in the twelfth century they now form one seventh of the population of India. The encounter between Islam and Hinduism has had lasting results and continue to be a major source of tension throughout the sub-continent.

In modern times Hinduism, instead of remaining static, has changed over the years by absorbing external influences, trends and innovations particularly from the west. Attitudes such as liberalism, humanism, technological advances and a scientific temper have been smoothly incorporated which exemplifies the ability of Hinduism to adopt new ideas

Rose petals adorn the marble fountain at Raj Vilas, Jaipur
(Previous page) Faithful gather for the prayer in seventeenth century mosque, the Jama Masjid, in Delhi

31

and adapt itself in the face of change. The social and intellectual questions raised by the Hindu thinkers like Raja Ram Mohan Roy and Mahatma Gandhi led to social reforms like widow remarriage and education of women. There was a concerted bid to introduce a new way of thinking. This led to the upsurge of both the revivalist and modernist movements.

While the traditional view was to shut out all change and blindly follow the pedantic principles of the religion the revivalist movement subjected Hinduism to a scrutiny that determined which elements of the religion needed to be preserved and which were to be rejected. An important consequence of this movement is that the sub-continent once more became a significant exporter of religions and religious ideas, although this time the flow was from the east to the west and not vice-versa as it was over two thousand years ago.

BUDDHISM

In the sixth century B.C. the excesses of Hinduism with its elaborate rituals and rigid caste system gave rise to two new philosophies, Buddhism and Jainism. Therefore these are basically offshoots of Hinduism.

Buddha or Siddharth Gautam as he was known as a young child, was born in Lumbini at the Nepal India border to a Kshatriya royal family. At an early age he showed an inclination towards meditation and reflection in the inner self. His father was displeased by his saintly behaviour. He wanted his son to lead his Sakya clan as a warrior. Buddha gave into the family wishes and got married. He had a son named Rahul from the marriage. Still the luxurious domestic life of the palace suffocated him. At the age of twenty one he became disillusioned with the worldly way of life and renounced it. He practiced yoga and engaged in radical asceticism. Finally he gave up these spiritual paths as fruitless and sat under the Bodhi tree in Bodhgaya and meditated for forty-five days. After a period of intense inner struggle, he attained enlightenment, which revealed the way of salvation from suffering. From then on he was known as the Buddha, the enlightened one. Buddha began to preach and delivered his first sermon in Sarnath near Varanasi. The text of this sermon contains the gist of Buddhism. He spoke of the Four Noble Truths and the eight- fold path.

Buddha questioned the Brahminical tradition and rejected the relevance of priests, Vedas, caste system, idol worship and elaborate rituals and sacrifices. Although he accepted the Hindu idea of *Karma*, of one's deeds in their present lives determining their next life. He returned briefly to his native town and converted his father, his wife, and other members of his family to his beliefs.

After forty five years of missionary activity Buddha died in Khusinagara, as a result of eating contaminated pork. He was about 80 years old.

Buddha's teachings were never written down during his lifetime. They continued to pass on by word of mouth for three hundred years. The teachings of Buddha were finally codified into canons or scriptures known as the *Tripatakas*.

The first religious meeting was held in Bodhgaya in the reign of King Ashoka. It was here that the monastic order or *Sangha* was founded. Texts began to be written first in *Prakrit* and then in *Pali*, the common language of the people.

Ashoka, the great Mauryan emperor, sought solace in Buddha's teachings. He was suffering remorse after his victory in the bloody battle of Kalinga, where his thirst for power had resulted in the death of thousands of innocent people. Ashoka's role was instrumental in spreading Buddha's message among his people. He had pillars, rocks and cave walls inscribed with his teachings all over the kingdom. Messengers carried the tenets of Buddhism to the Himalayan regions, Southeast Asia and even Greece.

Buddha's refusal to appoint a successor as head of the *Sangha* became a cause for disagreement and led to the division of the Buddhist community. After the death of Buddha his disciples split up in two sects, *Hinayana* and *Mahayana*.

Hinayana or the lesser vehicle was how Buddhism had actually started out. The followers of *Hinayana* believed in the monastic way of life. Buddha was represented through symbols like the wheel, feet, the Bodhi tree or an elephant. *Hinayana* continues to be a strong influence in Sri Lanka, Burma, Thailand, Laos and Cambodia.

Mahayana, the greater wheel of law gained more popularity, and bore some resemblance to Hinduism. It included the worship of statues of Buddha along with devotional rituals.

By the end of the twelfth century AD, Buddhism largely disappeared from India. The three main reasons that could have contributed to its disappearance appear to be: *Hinayana* offered little to the common people and gradually it lost its relevance as a spiritual force; the powerful resurgence of Hinduism under the patronage of the Hindu kings; and the Muslim invasions of India that led to large scale destruction of monasteries and Buddhist monks.

In India the places associated with Buddha's life continue to be major pilgrim centres even after two thousand six hundred years after Buddha's death.

JAINISM

Jainism is ascetically the most demanding of all the religions in India. Its purpose is not the glorification of an absolute God, but the attainment of self- perfection by the gradual abandonment of the material world.

Jain religion is centreed on the belief of an extreme form of *Ahimsa*, non- violence. One should never cause

(Opposite page) Dancer performing Theyyam, the religious dance drama of Kerala
(Following page left) Seventeenth century Basilica of Bom Jesus in Old Goa enshrines the tomb of St. Francis Xavier
(Following page right) A Sadhu poses for the photo outside the Orcha temple

33

harm to any living being, in action or speech. One should abstain from eating meat, and even vegetables like potatoes or onions, which are thought to harbor microscopic souls. To have possessions, fosters desire so one should give up all material things, even clothing. One should lead a life of celibacy and die through '*sallekhana*', a vow to fast until death.

Mahavira was the last tirthankar or prophet of the Jains, who lived in sixth century B.C. Like Buddha, he was of noble birth but renounced all worldly pleasures in search of knowledge. Mahavira's doctrine was similar to the teachings of Buddha in terms of release from desire, suffering and death. But whereas Buddha professed the Middle path between luxury and asceticism, Mahavira was of the belief that only severe asceticism and complete rejection of the material world can lead to salvation.

Mahavira travelled around India spreading the philosophy of non-violence. He rejected the caste system and was opposed to Bhramanical rituals. His simple teachings struck a cord with the masses that were greatly influenced by him.

There are two main sects of Jainism - *Digambar* and *Svetambar.*

Digambars or 'Sky-clad', are so called because their ascetics are completely naked and do not cover their bodies even in extreme weather conditions. They shave their heads, travel from place to place and eat only what is offered to them, and the amount of food eaten is what fits in their palms. All food is inspected before ingestion lest a life form comes to harm. They do not stay in one place for more than three days and the only thing they carry with them is a kamandal or a begging bowl and peacock feather fans. The latter is used for removing insects before they sit down to avoid killing them. In addition, they should avoid any speech, thought or action that incites or suggests violence.

The *Svetambars* or 'White-clad', wear only white robes. They too carry peacock feather fans and also wear a mask to prevent breathing in any organism. This sect accepts women nuns.

Jains are largely responsible for establishing vegetarianism as a desirable social practice and also gave Gandhi the basic notion of *Ahimsa*, used effectively in the freedom struggle. There are important Jain pilgrim centres in Bihar, Rajasthan, Gujarat and Mysore. The temples at Ranakpur and Dilwara in Rajasthan are of great beauty.

Paradoxically, the Jain community is the wealthiest in India. Because of religious restrictions they could not be farmers, for ploughing the fields would harm insects, or warriors since killing a human being is a transgression. The only option left to them was trading, with the result that the five million strong Jain community is disproportionately wealthy compared to the average population of India.

*Golden Temple in Amritsar is the holiest shrine for the Sikhs. It was built in the sixteenth century by Guru Arjan Dev, the fourth guru.
It is built in the middle of water tank called the pool of nectar. The early morning ceremony of the holy book, Guru Granth Sahib is
magical to witness*

A Jain pilgrim praying at the feet of the giant statue of Bahubali at Sravanabelagola in Karnataka
(Previous pages) Relatives in their traditional finery gather on the occasion of traditional Sikh wedding

ISLAM

Islam first took its roots in India with the coming of the Arab invaders in 711. Although it failed to make any significant impact in the beginning, the Afghans paved the way for the Delhi Sultanate to firmly establish it as a religion in India. The rulers of the Delhi Sultanate were of Turkish descent hailing from Central Asia, and had recently converted to Islam. They were dogmatic about preserving the purity of the Turkish race and perceived Islam not as a universal religion but as a colonial ideology of the ruling class.

The unrest in Central Asia around the thirteenth century resulted in a diaspora and huge numbers of migrants poured into India. These included people from all walks of life including soldiers, merchants, artisans and holy men. These migrants were mainly of Persian, Islamic and Afghan origin. They sought service with the Delhi Sultanate and its Mughal successors in North India. Although the trend of conversions to the Islamic faith had begun from the very first Arab conquest of Sindh followed by the Sultans of Delhi, it gained a new momentum during the Mughals.

Despite the conversions and migration of Muslims from Central Asia, they still comprised of a small minority. The majority consisted of non-Muslims and the rulers were pragmatic in dealing with them. Akbar was particularly conciliatory and banned cow-slaughter, abolished discriminatory taxes like *Jizyah* or pilgrim tax, encouraged Hindu-Muslim marriages and admitted Hindu scholars in his court.

Islam flowered during the reign of Akbar. Its advance could be seen in the architecture, which was a symbiosis of Hindu and Muslim styles, as well as literature and culture. His ideology was secular in nature. Islam found its converts mainly in the pre-agrarian nomads of north India and failed to make much headway in the Deccan and south India. Hindu peasants occupied these areas and coming of the Muslims did not make any significant socio-economic transformation in the rural society.

Muslim opinion was divided on the status of non- Muslims and ranged from outright acceptance to outright rejection.

Some were of the opinion that in order to fully understand Islam, studying the Hindu scriptures was imperative. They believed that all Hindus at some level believed in divine unity and that idol worship was a way of giving a tangible form to an abstract thought.

Some others took an extremist, discordant view and saw no connection between Islam and Hinduism. Unfortunately those adopting an extremist attitude outnumbered the ones with the conciliatory one.

The differences between Islam and Hinduism in terms of religious ideology and beliefs continue to be an area of concern in modern India.

SIKHISM

Sikhism started as a reform movement under the impact of the religious fundamentalism of Islam and Hinduism in medieval India.

Guru Nanak, [1469- 1539] the first Sikh guru, was the founder of Sikh religion. He was born in a Hindu family of Talwandi village near Lahore, where he worked as a shopkeeper. In 1500 his life changed by a vision in which God asked him to go out and spread the word of love and harmony.

Nanak embarked upon a series of wanderings and his contact with religious leaders of all persuasions made him realize the futility of complicated rituals and caste discrimination. He also rejected the orthodox Hindu and Muslim theories of attaining salvation. He was of the belief that God is omnipresent and within everyone and could not be restrained by temples or mosques.

The survival of Sikhism and its separate development owes much to the emphasis of Guru Nanak's hymns. They stress the need to practice a disciplined worldliness as an essential precondition for the manifestation of the divine grace.

Nanak's simple teachings appealed to the masses and are recorded in the holy book of Sikhs called the Guru Granth Sahib. The fifth Sikh guru, Arjan Dev, compiled the holy book and it is the only scripture in the world that has the distinction of being compiled by the founders of the religion during their lifetime. The Sikhs established a network of temples known as *Gurdwaras*, (abode of the Guru) which supported the voluntary free kitchens (*langar*) open to all. Guru Arjan Dev Singh also constructed the Golden Temple or Durbar Sahib in the city of Amritsar, which is the holiest place of Sikhism. There were nine more Gurus following Nanak.

Guru Govind Singh, the tenth Guru, initiated the Sikh baptism ceremony or the *Khalsa* order in the year 1699. The baptism vows include accepting a code of conduct.

The Khalsas have to observe their outward marks of orthodoxy called the Five K's. These include unshorn hair (*kesh*), a dagger (*kirpan*), a comb (*kangha*), a steel bangle (*kara*) and a pair of undergarment (*kachha*); a strict ban on consumption of tobacco; and the adoption of the common title of Singh, (lion) by men and Kaur, (princess) by women.

During the seventeenth century, the Khalsas were largely occupied in fighting persecution by Aurangzeb, the Mughal Emperor. Guru Teg Bahadur was beheaded in Chandni Chowk for opposing Aurangzeb's religious fundamentalism. Gurudwara Sis Ganj marks this spot of martyrdom.

The Sikhs are generally known as a hard working, happy-go-lucky community of India. They form only two percent of the total population and are mainly concentrated in Punjab.

CHRISTIANITY

Christianity has a long history in India. The Thomas Christians of Kerala claim St. Thomas the Apostle of Jesus Christ, as their founder. Although written evidence is lacking it is widely believed in south India that the saint was martyred in Tamil Nadu. This is the popular version, though there are others who believe St. Bartholomew was the first missionary to visit India.

There is evidence to suggest the presence of Christianity in Kerala from the sixth century, when the Nestorian church started its missionary work overseas. The priests and traders from Syria may have been responsible for bringing Christianity to Kerala. There is a strong Syrian influence as the liturgy of the Thomas Christians was in Syria, their doctrine Nestorian and they owed their allegiance to the Syrian Patriarch.

However, the Christians could not remain aloof of the Hindu influence. The Thomas Christians were indifferent to the lower castes, and held a high status.

Goa became the centre of Portuguese missionary activities in Asia under St. Francis Xavier, whose tomb in Goa is a pilgrimage centre for thousands of Christians. Jesuit missionaries were sent from Goa to the Mughal court and engaged in religious debates under Akbar's tolerant encouragement.

There were many conversions in Goa and its neighborhood, and the missionaries were especially active further south. Entire fishing communities of Tamil Nadu, Kerala and Sri Lanka converted to Christianity. Missionaries succeeded St. Francis from Germany, Denmark, Holland and Britain.

The evangelical revival stimulated Protestant missionary activity in the nineteenth century. Three functions were soon identified and generally accepted among the missionaries. These were preaching, teaching and healing. Christian schools, colleges and hospitals sprung up all over India including remote and backward areas. They played an important role in the spread of education and helped women and tribals immensely by their influence.

Christianity has played a vital role in shaping modern India. Despite the humanitarian work carried out by the Christian missionaries, there remained some suspicion of Christianity being a foreign import. They were accused of being anti-national and carrying out forcible conversions. However, to the credit of the Christian missionaries, they have always maintained a non-confrontational attitude and are primarily engaged in social improvement by education and social reform.

The impact of Christianity is evident in the fact that Mahatma Gandhi incorporated the teachings of Jesus Christ into the efforts to free India during the freedom struggle.

Today Christians in India remain a small but growing minority. The Protestants are growing more than the Roman Catholics and the greatest increase both in number and proportion is in south India.

ZOROASTRIANISM

Parsis are the followers of the ancient Persian religion called Zoroastrianism. The religion was founded by prophet Zoroaster in 1555 B.C. His teachings form part of the sacred scripture called Zend — Avestha.

Darius I, Xerxes I, and Artaxerxes II were the Persian kings under whose patronage the religion flourished. Artaxerxes II is also credited in building the first Zoroastrian temples around 390 B.C. Later the Sassanid dynasty of Persia established Zoroastrianism as the state religion.

The Parsis or Zoroastrians first landed at the west coast of India, after the Muslim conquest of their homeland, Persia in the eighth century. Jadirana, the local king, was worried as to how his limited resources would support such a large influx of immigrants. It is said that the leader of the Parsis asked for a glass of water and added a spoonful of sugar in it. The water level remained the same although it tasted sweeter; the Parsis would assimilate themselves in a similar fashion, without disturbing the local population, explained the leader. The local king agreed to give them shelter but on three conditions. They would learn to speak the local language, dress in local clothes and would not allow the locals into their temples. The local Gujarati population gave the Parsis their name, which means those from Persia.

Their places of worship are called the Fire Temples or *Agyari*, where they pray in front of the holy fire that represents purity and truth. They believe in an omnipres-

Faithful gather for the afternoon prayer in Jama Masjid in Old Delhi . It was built by the fifth Mughal emperor Shah Jahan
(Opposite page) Mughal motifs painted in the palace of Amer

*Thousands of Hindu pilgrims gather for the holy bath in the river Ganges
on the occasion of Maha Kumbh at Har ki Pauri in Haridawar
(Previous pages) A Naga sadhu with his chela or apprentice returning from the Maha Kumbh Mela,
camp temporarily on the banks of the Ganges*

ent god Ahura Mazda and of the eternal conflict between the good and the evil, represented by Spenta Mainyu and Angra Mainyu respectively. Initiation rites (*Navjote*) are done before the puberity in which a sacred shirt (*dusti*) and sacred thread is presented.

Parsis pray five times a day and offer their allegiance to the Good Religion of God, Ahura Mazdi. Earth, fire and water are held sacred in their religion and Death is the work of evil. Since all decaying, dead matter represents evil, they place their corpses in the *Doxma* or Tower of Silence, where vultures eat up the mortal remains.

Zoroastrian practice has remained remarkably faithful over the centuries although its interpretation and doctrines have undergone change. *Ilm-I-Kshnoom* or 'Path of Knowledge' is the philosophy they adhere to.

The Parsi population has declined because of low birthrate and also because they cannot marry outside their faith, as they do not accept any converts. The children of such inter- religious marriages are also not allowed to become Parsis.

As the economic opportunities increased under the British rule in Bombay, the city was to become their new home. It is here where the majority of them reside (about 100,000). Due to their western appearance and eating habits the British readily accepted Parsis. Their straightforward honest dealings soon earned them a good name in the business world. The Parsi family, Tata is a household name in India, industrialists well known for free enterprise, integrity and vision in business. They are the pioneers in the field of steel, automobiles, aviation, hospitality, chemicals etc. Many Parsis have also excelled in the field of science and music.

JUDAISM

India has attracted a wealth of visitors from various countries through its trade routes, including Jews from many parts of the Middle East and Europe. Another factor was the Nazi genocide, which brought a wave of Jewish immigrants to the sub-continent. The religious tolerance of India assimilated any faith with open arms.

Judaism has never been a widespread religion in India, although there is evidence to believe that its existence in India is at least as old as Christianity. The three main communities, which continue to live here, although in very small numbers, are the Cochin Jews or white Jews of Kerala, with Malayalam as their mother toungue, the Bene Israel on the west coast, near Bombay. The Bagdadis have Marathi language as their mother toungue. They have preserved old customs, which were evolved down the centuries living in relative isolation from rest of the Jewish world.

The Jewish community, numbered 30,000 when India declared Independence in 1947. It has shrunk considerably in recent years with most Jews opting to leave for their homeland in Israel or to head for other countries in search of better economic prospects.

destinations

Dramatic view of the Lamayuru monastery in remote Ladakh as seen from the neighbouring mountain
(Previous page) Confluence of the Indus and Zanzkar rivers at Nimmu in the mountainous region of Ladakh
(Following page) Three Kashmiris dressed in their Firans, the traditional gowns, returning home after selling their goods
in the floating vegetable market of the Dal Lake in Srinagar

Leh and Srinagar are two most important cities of the northern Himalayan state of Jammu and Kashmir. They lie nestled in the Great Himalayan, Ladakh, Zanskar, Karakoram and Pir Panjal ranges bordering with Pakistan to the west and China to the east.

Ladakh-the name itself means the land of high mountain passes-lies between the mighty folds of the Himalayan ranges. Due to its location in the rain shadow region of the Himalayas, its barren landscape (often termed as the moon land) is full of awe-inspiring

some vegetation is possible in the river valley to sustain its thin population. Mongol nomads, Dards and the Mons were the earliest settlers in the region. Together with the Muslim traders, who arrived in the seventeenth century, they makeup the ethnic fabric of Ladakh.

Leh is the capital city of Ladakh lies at the altitude of three thousand five hundred meters in the valley of the river Indus. The surrounding high mountains provide a spectacular backdrop to the fifteenth century Dard fortress and palace that dominates its skyline. The town

SRINAGAR, LEH, LADAKH

mountains and snow-fed rivers and valleys. The only means of communication for its hardy but extremely polite inhabitants are the high mountain passes, and during the winter months when the passes are snowbound, the frozen bed of Zanskar river is only means of communication in the region devoid of roads.

The important regions of Ladakh are Nubra to the north, Zanskar to the south, Balti to the west and fertile valley of Indus river to nestled to east. In the summer months

came into prominence when Sengge Namgyal shifted the capital from Shey in 1879. Its broad bazaar was an important halt for the caravans carrying merchandise on the silk and wool route. The Chinese occupation of Tibet put an end to this flourishing trade.

Today the economy is sustained by tourism (which opened only in 1974) in the summer months. The Indian army, which has the daunting task of guarding the frozen frontier, is the backbone of the local economy. Leh is a

popular base for most of the excursions to the exotic monasteries that are situated along the river Indus. The Shanti stupa on the edge of the town provides a picturesque view of Leh.

In the eleventh century there was a surge in temple building in Ladakh, which can be attributed to Rinchen Tsampo, popularly known as "the translator". He was directly responsible of translating the Indian Buddhist texts and propagating the religion in Ladakh. Many of the temples and monasteries date back to this period.

Southeast of Leh, on the Manali highway is the Hemis monastery. Isolated and hidden in Shang valley, it is world famous for its mask dance festival Tsichu, held in the month of June or July to celebrate the birth of Buddhist Guru Padmasambhava. It is one of the few Ladakhi festivals held in the summer months.

Thikse is to Ladakh what Patola Palace is to Tibet. Palden Sherab founded the *gonpa* (monastery) in the fifth century. It situated on a high hill in the Indus valley. Three huge *chortens* (stupa) mark its entrance. It boasts of a large monastery of hundred monks and a library with ancient manuscripts. There are numerous temples at various levels of the *gonpa*. A temple with a fifteen-meter high gold coloured statue of Lord Buddha was added as recently as 1980. It was inaugurated Dalai Lama, the spiritual head of Tibetan Buddhists.

It is fascinating to explore various levels of this white washed gonpa in which the older *dukhang* (prayer halls) have some beautiful *thangkas* (Tibetan Buddhist cloth paintings) and murals painted on the walls. The view from the roof is equally impressive with the green expanse irrigated by the river Indus on the left of the road and stark desert on the opposite side littered with white washed *chortens* that give it a surreal aura.

To the northwest of Leh are another set of beautiful monasteries and temples. Notable among them are Spituk, Alchi, Rizong and Lamayuru. Spituk is fifteenth century monastry of yellow cap sect of Tibetan Buddhist called Gelugpa. It is situated at the end of the runway of Leh airport, which incidentally is the highest in the world.

Alchi is situated in the fertile river basin of river Indus is considered as one of the important archaeological heritage sites of India. It is a group of five sacred *gonpas* out of which Sumstek (three story *gonpa*) is the most important as it houses most important images of Avalokitesvara, Maitreya and Manjusri of incredible size. The temples are not as imposing as the others in the region but the frescoes and the wooden sculptures they contain date back nearly a millennium. These are a treasure trove of unique Mahayana Buddhist art of the world.

Lamayuru is a three-hour ride to the west of Leh. The drive is richly rewarded with some exotic scenery of Ladakh as the road winds its way along the river Indus.

The deep gorges of the river and its confluence with Zanskar river are some of the highlights of the trip. Mountains of every conceivable hue and texture are among the visual delights that one experiences as one after another breathtaking views unfold in front of the eyes. Lamayuru is itself situated on a steep cliff nestled by Zanskar mountains, which look like a lunar landscape. It perhaps is the most photogenic *gonpa* of Ladakh. Surrounding mountains offer some superb views of the monastery and the small village situated at the bottom of the cliff.

The Tibetan Buddhist sect of Kagyupa manages Lamayuru monastery. It dates back to medieval times when the caravans of the silk route would halt there. The structure we see today dates back to sixteenth century. The dukhang or the prayer hall has an image of one thousand armed *Avalokitesvara* — or one whose life was dedicated to the service of mankind. Today it is the gateway to treks in the Zanskar valley.

Ladakh, the land between the earth and sky, is the last surviving bastion of Tibetan Buddhism of the world after the occupation of Tibet by communist China.

SRINAGAR

"If there is a paradise on this earth, it is here, it is here, and it is here". Although these words are written in gold in the Red Fort of Delhi, they aptly describe the beauty of Kashmir Valley. This fertile region is situated between the Pir Panjal and the Great Himalayas range. The capital city of the valley is Srinagar where life revolves around the river Jhelum and the lakes of Dal and Nagin. The valley is lush green with paddy and saffron fields. Apples, pears and walnut orchards abound the region. Chinar trees show their majestic beauty in the famous Mughal Gardens, which were laid out by the ruling Mughal dynasty to escape the hot plains of the north India in the summer months. During the Raj or colonial rule, the British too, like the Mughals, escaped to Kashmir and resided in the famous houseboats, which are anchored in the waters of Dal and Nagin Lakes.

Houseboats are the floating hotels richly carved out from the local walnut wood and decorated with locally made silk carpets and tapestry. All this is set dramatically in the beautiful backdrop of the snow-capped mountains. It is an exhilarating experience to cruise in the canals of the lake in local boats with heart-shaped oars called shikaras. The oldest monuments in the region are the sun temples of Martand, built by the Karkota dynasty in eighth century.

Sadly today this paradise of blooming flowers and gliding shikaras in crystalline lakes is out of bounds for the tourists as it is in the grip of religious fundamentalists.

The entrance door of a Buddhist temple

Young lamas head for the Dukhang in Lamayuru
(Opposite page) Buddhist monks on the terrace of Thiksey Monastery with fabulous views of the snow capped mountains and the
river Indus in the background

Ladakhi women in typical hats and men dressed in their traditional attire await for the arrival reception of Dalai Lama

Golden statue of Maitreya Buddha in Thiksey gompa, Ladakh
(Opposite page) View of the Spituk Dukhang where monks pray in front of Buddhas image
(Previous page) Locals crowd in the courtyard of the Lamayuru monastery
and the roof tops of neighbouring houses to witness the unfurling of the giant thanka (religious painting)

Panoramic view of the Kailasha Temple at Ellora caves near Aurangabad.
The temple is a monolithic structure of gigantic scale. It is carved out of an entire mountain
by chisel and hammer in the eighth century

Bombay is the commercial capital of India. The city which is less than 500 years old since its 'discovery' by the Portuguese, has metamorphosed into a sprawling megalopolis of thirteen million people. Bombay is India's most dynamic and westernized city. It does not have a distinct regional character because of its mixed population. The separate identity each community maintains has given rise to a mix of places of worship, customs and

of Braganza's dowry when she married Charles II. A few years later in 1668 it was leased to the East India Company for a pittance. The city grew in importance with the opening of the railways in the nineteenth century, and its natural harbor became an international port of call with the construction of the Suez Canal in 1869. The Civil War in America caused the cotton supplies to shrink in the world market. This proved to be the boon in disguise for the city. Millions were made

BOMBAY, GOA, AURANGABAD, AJANTA, ELLORA

rituals, making it very cosmopolitan.

In 1996 Bombay was renamed Mumbai, which is the Marathi name of a local deity. It is also the film capital of India with the largest film industry in the world.

Mumbai originally consisted of seven islands inhabited by small Koli fishing communities. The Portuguese handed the largest island of Bom Bain (Good Bay) to the English in 1661, as part of Catherine

as the city was located close to the cotton-producing region and had a natural port to boast of. The Gothic buildings which dominate the Bombay's skyline date from this period.

Subsequently Mumbai rapidly became the centre of an entrepreneurial as well as a commercial class, drawing from the Parsis as well as Bania and Gujarati business community. The small Parsi community has been instrumental in the development of the Indian industry with the result that Tatas are a household name in India. The family gave Bombay its landmark, the Taj Mahal hotel. Built in Edwardian style by Chambers in 1903, it is still regarded as one of the finest hotels of the world.

Besides the Maharashtrian, Gujarati and Christian communities there is also a small minority of Jews and Parsis. The influence of the various cultures existing simultaneously is evident in the architecture of the city. Unlike Delhi, which is sprinkled with ruins of the Muslim dynasties, it is the British landmarks that stand out in Bombay. Prime among them is the Gateway of India. It was designed by George Wittet to commemorate the visit of King George V and Queen Mary in 1911. Ironically, it was through this very arch that the last contingent of British troops (1st Battalion Somerset Light Infantry) in India left by sea in 1948. Wittet also built the Prince of Wales Museum.

The Victoria Terminus also popularly known as VT was built in the last quarter of the nineteenth century by F.W. Stevens. It is a truly remarkable Victorian Gothic style building. The numerous sculptures decorating its façade were designed by Thomas Earp and executed by the students of the Arts College. A visit to the Victoria Terminus will give a taste of the pulsating energy of the city. Other colonial buildings include Old Secretariat, Crawford Market, the Municipal building.

More than the architecture, it is the sea, which surrounds the city on three sides that dominates the cultural consciousness of the city and dictates its lifestyles. Beaches and seaside promenades like Marine Drive, Chowpatti and Juhu beach, and the outlying resorts of Madh Island, Marve, Manori and Gorai, though eaten into by the spread of urban expansion, are still the visitor's delight.

Mumbai is also the departure point for the Elephanta caves. This enchanting island, an hour away by motor launch, offers a welcome getaway from the chaos of the city. There are a series of beautiful rock cut caves with temples and sculptures dating back to sixth century. The island was named by the Portuguese in honour of the carved elephant they found at the port. Its chief attraction is the unique cave temple, which houses a six-meter high bust of Shiva in his three manifestations as Creator, Preserver and Destroyer.

Mumbai is the most prosperous city in the country, with a cost of living almost equal to that in the US, and houses some of the most expensive properties in the world. However, poverty continues to be a growing vice with one-third of Mumbai's population living in slums or shantytowns. Despite communal tensions and a growing mafia nexus posing a grave threat to the city, Mumbai maintains its status as the financial, commercial and entertainment capital of India.

AURANGABAD, AJANTA & ELLORA

The city of Aurangabad was originally known as Khadki. It was founded by Malik Amber in the year 1610. Later it was named after Aurangzeb, the sixth Mughal ruler, who made this town a base for his expansion in the Deccan region. Aurangabad is known for its monuments like the Bibi-Ka-Muqbara, a poor imitation of the Taj Mahal. Prince Azam Shah built it in 1678 in the memory of his mother Begum Rabia Daurani, queen of the emperor Aurangzeb. The tomb shows the decline in the Mughal architecture in the span of just 25 years as compared to the Taj Mahal in Agra. The invincible Daulatabad fort and Aurangzeb's burial spot at Khuldabad are not far away. As places of interest these are overshadowed by the Ajanta and Ellora caves nearby, which are now declared as world heritage monuments.

Ajanta caves are situated in a horse-shoe shaped valley of the river Wagdogra, 65 miles (105 km) northeast from Aurangabad. Its serene surroundings and the proximity to the trade routes made it the centre of Buddhist art and philosophy from the second century B.C. till the sixth century A.D. There are around thirty caves on the Deccan plateau that were excavated in two distinct phases. The earlier *Hinayana* phase in which Buddha was worshipped only through symbols such as *Bodhi* tree, footprints and *stupas*. In the later Mahayana period Buddha was worshipped in human form. The caves of the *Mahayana* period introduced Buddha idols in place of stupas of the *Hinayana* period.

The Ajanta caves were lost to the civilization for over a thousand years. A British soldier, John Smith, accidentally discovered them in 1820, while he was in pursuit of a tiger. Being lost to the civilization for centuries proved a boon in disguise for these temples and monasteries as they escaped defacement from marauding invaders.

The caves at Ajanta show the transition of the temple architecture from wood to that of stone. In many roofs the imitation of wooden beams is apparent (cave no. 19). The temples were carved out of cliff face from front to the back then from top to bottom. The caves are divided into the *Chaityas*, the prayer halls and *Viharas*, the monasteries. Tempera paintings that decorate the walls and ceilings of some caves are narrative in nature and richly depict the daily life as well as the epic stories of Buddhism. Although only four colours namely red, blue, yellow ochre and lampblack were used, the paintings emerge as vivid and expressive along with strong composition.

The rough walls of the caves were covered with an inch thick plaster made out of clay and cow dung and portions of rice husk were added. Once the plaster dried a layer of lime plaster was applied. The

14

outlines of the paintings were done in red on wet plaster. The colours used were locally procured except the blue, which was imported; hence it has been used in small quantities. Pools of water were made in order to reflect the sunlight in the darkest corners of the caves for the artists to work.

The earlier *Hinayana* paintings are simple by nature and mostly two-dimensional. The later *Mahayana* paintings are highly stylized where the artist have used the depth in the perspective and covered the entire walls with the *Jatakas*, the stories related to the earlier incarnation of Buddha as *Bodhisattva*. These are beautifully illustrated in vivid colours and life like vibrancy. These paintings depict colourful Buddhist legends of divinities with an exuberance and vitality that is unsurpassed in Indian art. The noteworthy being the painting of the Bodhisattva Padamapani, the lotus bearer in cave number one. The sensual and spiritual blend in painting art is beautifully accomplished in the cave temples of Ajanta more than fifteen hundred years ago.

About thirty kilometers from Aurangabad, close to the fort of Daulatabad, lie the Ellora caves. In all thirty four cave temples were excavated between the fifth and eleventh centuries. Unlike Ajanta, which is purely Buddhist, the Ellora caves are mixture of Buddhist, Hindu and Jain religions. The Buddhist caves are the oldest and pertain to Mahayana sect who started the idol worship. In contrast to the Ajanta caves, the existence of Ellora was known to the local population. Being situated on ancient trade route, it has been referred as Verul in accounts of the Arab traders. It is estimated that for the construction of these temples some 200,000 tons of rock was excavated. Out of the thirty four caves, twelve belong to Mahayana Buddhism, and date from fifth to the seventh century. These are located towards the south. Seventeen Hindu caves date from eighth to the ninth century lie in the centre. In the north are the remaining five Jain caves, which were constructed between the ninth to the eleventh century.

Out of the numerous Viharas or the monasteries made in the Buddhist group *"teen tal"* or the three storeys one is most amazing. Compared to the Hindu caves, the Buddhist caves are quite simple. Hindu caves are adorned with the dynamic statues of the various gods and goddess, representative of the dynamic energy. The zenith of temple architecture at Ellora is cave number sixteen, the Kailasha Temple, named after the lofty Himalayan Mountain abode of lord Shiva. Unlike other caves, which were excavated inside the mountain from the front to the back, in Kailasha an entire mountain was chiseled to leave a giant temple, probably the biggest monolithic temple in the world, carved out of an entire mountain.

Construction of the Kailasha temple began in the eighth century, beginning in the reign of Krsna I, (Krishna I; 756 - 773) of the Rashtrakuta dynasty. It took about ninety-three years to be completed. It involved the removal of three million cubic feet of solid rock to form a temple that is 276 feet long, 154 feet wide, and 107 feet deep, with four levels, or storeys. Despite of its giant size, it is elaborately carved.

Just at the entrance, in the porch is the beautiful carving of Laxmi, Hindu goddess of prosperity, seated on the floating lotus. The base of the main shrine is twenty-five feet high and is supported by life size carvings of elephants from the outside. The best of friezes is of the ten-headed demon king Ravana shaking Kailasha. It narrates the incident from the Hindu epic Ramayana when the demon king Ravana, intoxicated with his strength, shakes the mount Kailasha where Shiva is residing with his consort Parvati. Although Parvati looks alarmed by the incident, Shiva on the other hand suppresses the giant with a gentle tap of his foot.

Another carving which reflects the dynamic energy of these sculptures is that of Vishnu in Narsimha, half man-lion avatar, killing the demon Hiranyakasipu. The narration of Ramayana in a frieze is another remarkable panel.

The glory of the temple is aptly described in the words of Percy Brown, an authority on Indian architecture, "Kailasha temple is an illustration of one of those rare moments when men's mind and heart work in unison towards the consummation of a supreme ideal".

(Opposite page) Fifth century painting of Bodhisattva Padmapani or the lotus bearer decorating the walls of Cave No. 1, at Ajanta caves near Aurangabad
(Following page) Gateway of India built for the reception of King George the fifth, has welcomed travellers and traders since 1911. Here it is seen from the Taj Mahal Hotel, another important landmark of Bombay

*Victoria Terminus, popularly known as VT, is a classical example of Victorian Gothic architecture which dominated Bombay's
skyline in the last quarter of the nineteenth century
(Opposite page) Dhobighat – Place where the laundryman cleans the clothes collected from the thousands of households,
he dries and irons each item before returning it to rightful owner. A few dots and bars are the codes that mark the ownership
of each garment which only the dhobi (laundryman) can decipher
(Following page) Goa is the holiday paradise for the locals and the visitors, this old Portuguese colony has a perfect blend of east and west.
Beautiful churches, golden beaches and colourful markets are among the many attractions here*

*Miracle of Swarsati or hundred manifestations of Buddha, is a remarkable carving executed in the antechamber
of cave no. 7 that dates back to the fifth century, at Ajanta*
(Opposite page) A fifth century painting in the verandah of Cave No. 17 at Ajanta, shows Indira accompanied by heavenly beauties and musicians
*(Previous page) Seventh century, 23 feet long sculpture of Buddha depicting Mahaparinirvana, or Buddha's release from the cycle of rebirth,
in bas-relief below are the worldly possessions of Buddha and mourning disciples. Ajanta, Cave No 26*
*(Page before previous page) An hour's ride on the launch from Gateway of India, takes one to eighth century Elephanta Caves.
The caves are rock cut temples excavated on the face of the mountain. The panels inside depict important legends from Shiv Puranas*

*School excursion at Ellora where the children admire
the world's largest monolithic temple chiseled out of an entire mountain as seen above*

Fifteenth century Jain tirath or pilgrimage centre at Ranakpur. It is located in picturesque isolated spot surrounded by Aravalli mountains. It is executed entirely in white marble replicating the celestial vehicle on earth. The sikhars or the temple towers adorned with prayer flags look impressive against the clouded sky
(following pages) A marble panel from Ranakpur temple showing images of nine tirthankars

Udaipur is the seat of Maharanas of Mewar who belong to the Sisodia clan of Rajputs, the oldest ruling family of India. The title Maharana was given to them for they never surrendered in a battle. Nor did they accept the dominance of any foreign rule, either of the Muslims or of the British. As a mark of respect they were the chiefs of thirty-six clans of Rajputs. Although the Sisodias were defeated, they always sprung back to avenge their honour.

Their kingdom has a rich history of resistance to

empty chair belonged to Maharana Fateh Singhji of Udaipur, whose displeasure at British rule was well known. The chair, which signified the Rajput sense of pride, is still on display at the City Palace. The Maharanas of Mewar can trace their family to Bapa Rawal of 728, who received the state of Mewar in trust from his mentor Guru Harit Rashi, at Eklingji. It is the oldest ruling family of India or perhaps of the world. Bapa Rawal established his capital in Chittor, which once was the largest fortified city in the world. The repeated siege of Chittor made the Maharanas

UDAIPUR, RANAKPUR, DILWARA

the Muslims. The surrounding areas of Haldighati, Chittor and Kumbhalgarh bear testimony to the fierce battles between the Rajputs and the Mughals. The legends of warrior kings Rana Sangha and Rana Pratap are still sung by the people of the area. The Sisodias of Mewar are also proud of the fact that they never gave their daughters to the Mughal harem.

The long and turbulent history of the Rajputs also includes defiance of the British. As late as 1911 when the Delhi Durbar was held to honour George V, the only

move to more ideally situated and naturally defended city in the sixteenth century.

Udaipur can easily be called as the romantic city of India. It is the city of lakes and gardens, with majestic palaces on the fringes of the lake. The city is most famous for its fairy tale Lake Palace situated in the middle of Lake Pichola. The palace was originally known as Jagat Vilas. It was a pleasure island made out of white marble and delicately decorated in bright coloured crystal. It took three years to be completed and was inaugurated in the year 1746. The inauguration ceremony was well attended by the ladies from the royal family and hundreds of concubines accompanying them.

Some two hundred years later it was converted into a luxury hotel. Among its first guests was Queen Elizabeth II. To this day Who's Who of the world make it to this enchanted island where one is ferried across by boat to this unique hotel. The ride is breathtaking especially when one sees the palaces on the edge of the lake reflected in the water. The City Palace, the residence of Maharana of Udaipur, is at the other end of the lake Pichola. The older part of the palace has been made into a museum, which contains the largest collection of Mewari paintings, while another section is now the Shiv Niwas Palace, a luxury hotel. The new part of the palace is known as the Fateh Prakash Palace and houses some of the finest crystal collections of the nineteenth century. The balcony overlooking the lake provides stunning views of the Lake Palace.

The surrounding Aravalli hills have beautiful forts, palaces and temples, which are worth exploring. Eklingji temple is the "*kul devta*" of the Maharanas of Mewar, nearby are the temples of Nagdha. Close by is Devigarh, a beautiful fort that has been lovingly restored into a luxury hotel.

DILWARA

About four hours drive to the east is the Dilwara Temple located in the Rajasthan's only hill station, Mt. Abu. At Dilwara there are five Svetambar Jain temples dating from twelve to the fourteenth century. The Vimal Vashi and Luna Vashi temples are the biggest and most beautiful. The first temple is named after its builder Vimal Shah, who was the general in the army of the king Bhimdev. In his final years Vimal Shah's guru encouraged him to build a temple to repent for his sins.

The temple was constructed in 1077. It took 180 million rupees, 14 years with 1500 workers and 1200 labourers to construct the temple. The marble was quarried from nearby Ambaji mines. It is easy to believe the local folklore, which explains how the artisans chiseled out incredible carvings in marble. The dust, which came out of the carving, was weighed in equal amounts with gold and for broken pieces the silver was used for payment. Hence it is no wonder that the artisans gave the world one of the most beautiful temples unmatched in any part of the world. The sculpture adorned the temples with delicately carved human, animal and floral motifs, which makes the hard marble appear as fine as porcelain. The other temple, Luna Vashi is

dedicated to Lord Neminath and was built about two hundred years after Vimal Vashi temple. Two small temples flanking the sanctum are incredible in carving. They are the result of the competition between the mother-in-law and her daughter-in-law. The columns and the carvings on the roof depicting the mythological stories are mesmerizing.

RANAKPUR

Three hours drive through the scenic Aravali Mountains is Ranakpur, one of the finest examples of temple architecture of medieval India. Seth Dharan Shah, who was minister in the court of Rana Kumbha, constructed it in the early fifteenth century. The inspiration came for it from the dream of the minister in which he saw *Nalini-glum vimana*, a celestial vehicle for the Gods. Afterwards Seth Dharan Shah spoke to Maharana of Mewar and expressed his desire to make a temple. Rana was quick to encourage him and granted him a beautiful secluded spot on the banks of the river Maghai. As the mark of respect to the king the name Ranakpur was given to this sacred site.

The architect named Deepa translated the dream into reality. He understood the plan, which was in Dharan Shah's dream. The work was started in the year 1439 and the original plan was to build it seven storeys high. But keeping in mind the failing health of its patron the temple was inaugurated in the year 1499. It was dedicated to the first Jain prophet, Adinath.

The inner sanctum is unique in India as it has four statues of Adinath, the first of the twenty-four Jain prophets. 2500 sculptors worked on the site and the temple was completed after 63 years. The temple is three storeys high and has four doors to enter. Each storey the temple is adorned with four-faced statue of the prophet. The domes and the torans are profusely decorated with fine marble sculptures. There are said to be 1444 columns of which no two are alike. In respect to the almighty lord one column has been left crooked so that the perfection can only rest with the divine. Once you enter the temple the Dharan Shah's dream can be seen carved out in white marble. There is a popular Jain saying which goes as:

> "The fine sculpture of Dhilwara,
> The architecture of Ranakpur,
> Lofty height of Tarangaji,
> And serenity of Shatruanjaya,
> So, my faithful
> Even though you have to eat less,
> You must visit these holy temples"

Jag Mandir, a seventeenth century pleasure island of Udaipur Maharana reflecting in the serene waters of lake Pichola also seen floating is Gangaur, the party boat of Maharana

Colourful attire is the characteristic of the state of Rajasthan. In order to compensate the lack of colour in their arid landscape, men adorn themselves with colorful turbans while women attire themselves in vibrant skirts and scarfs (lehenga odhni)

(Opposite page) Luxuriously decorated suite in eighteenth century Lake Palace in contrast with traditionally decorated seventeenth century suite of the City Palace in Udaipur (above)

(Opposite page & above) Adinatha Temple at Ranakpur is decorated with intricately carved idols and columns of which no two are alike
(Following pages) Neminatha or Luna Vashi temple at Dilwara, with its exquisitely carved ceiling of rangmandapa in lotus design. The carvings on columns
and serpentine torans or arches surpass any such attempt in the country. The artisans were encouraged by the patrons to carve as deftly as they could   95
because the dust taken out from these carvings was weighed and artisans got paid in equal amount of gold

White marble memorial built in the memory of Maharaja Jaswant Singh II of Jodhpur glows in the twilight
(Following page) Painted window in Jaisalmer Fort

The first ruler of Marwar is said to be Sheoji. He was the great grandson of Jaichand, the ruler of Kanauj. In the twelfth century the invading Muslim armies of the Mamluks dynasty pushed Sheoji out of Kanauj. He escaped to Marwar, the land of the dead, where he finally took shelter in its vast desert. Later his descendants gained control of the area. Rao Jodha, the Rathore king, built Jodhpur in the year 1459. Jodha was only a young boy when his father was killed by the Sisodia clan at Chittor. The Sisodias drove the young monarch into the

food is a lot cooler". The old lady was right thought Jodha. He started conquering the villages on the outskirts.

Finally the clans of Sisodias and the Rathores sat down to demarcate their boundaries. Where the Anola, bright yellow flower shrub grew was to be the Sisodias, land and where thorny Baoliya grew was to be Rathore land. This demarcation is quite evident when one drives from Udaipur to Jodhpur. On his return to Mandore, Rao Jodha decided to have a secure capital. Bhakurcheeria hill was chosen as the site. A man

JODHPUR, JAISALMER, BIKANER

desert and captured Mandore. For over ten years young Maharaja wandered about trying to win back his kingdom. An interesting incident changed his destiny.

One day, Rao Jodha, dying of hunger, entered an old lady's hut. Seeing the young man famished, the humble lady served him piping hot "*khichri*," a mixture of lentils and boiled rice. He took a helping of hot dish and burned his tongue. Seeing his suffering the old lady said: "You are just like Jodha, who also always attacks in the centre of the kingdom; always start from the edges where the

was buried alive to counter the curse of the sadhu who was displaced from there.

The original entrance was where the stone engraving marks "Rao Jodha's Falsa". Opposite to it, is a smaller slab in the memory of the heroic deed of Rajiya Bambi, who was buried alive in the foundation of the fort. For this great service the royal family still gives due respect to the descendants of the family. Chamunda Devi statue was installed at the edge of the fort, for the warring Rajputs whose battles cry is "Ranbanka Rathore" invincible in battle. Later, gates and chambers were added to this majestic fortified palace. It was occupied by the Rathores for four hundred years right up to Maharaja Jaswant II in the late nineteenth century. At the final entrance to the palace, one is greeted by the shehnai players, on the either side of this gate are the palm marks of the queens who immolated themselves on their husbands' funeral pyre, a medieval act of sati, which has long been discontinued.

The fort now houses an excellent collection of Marwar paintings, Mughal *howdas* (the elephant seats), palanquins, cradles, royal tents and arms. The *jharokas* of the palace provide a panoramic view of the blue city or the *Brahmnagri*, the living quarters of the Brahmins.

The other important landmark of the city is the Umaid Bhavan Palace, the last royal residence to be built in the country. The foundation of the palace was laid on top of Chhittar hill in 1929 and the palace was finally inaugurated in 1944. By building it, Maharaja Umaid Singh provided employment to the thousands of citizens, suffering under drought. The British architect Mr. Lanchanshire was chosen to design the building. It is built entirely of rose-coloured sandstone, which was quarried locally and white Makrana marble. The Viceroy's Palace in New Delhi inspired the use of the stone. Lanchanshire was also on the board of consultants for building New Delhi. Tongue and groove method was employed to build the structure. An ice factory was built close by so that heavy blocks that could not be lifted, even by crane, were slipped into place on blocks of ice. It is probably the finest example of art deco anywhere in the world. It is still the royal residence while part of it is a luxury hotel.

The palace boasts of a swimming pool in its basement, marble squash courts, billiards room and a theatre for the royal family. The lawns on the western side of the palace are flanked by the various hues of bougainvillea shrubs. Sitting in the veranda watching the sunset is an unforgettable experience. Maharaja Umaid Singh did not rest after building the palace for himself. He also constructed a public hospital, school, dams, irrigation canals, and a road network. He modernized the desert capital without disturbing the fabric of local culture.

Jaswant Thada is the royal cenotaph made out of white Makrana marble in the memory of Jaswant Singh II in the later part of the nineteenth century. There are smaller cenotaphs of the other members of the royal family.

Just a few miles away from the city are the Mandore gardens. These house the royal cenotaphs of the Maharajas. They have some beautiful memorials of the earlier members of the royal family. The largest and finest of all cenotaphs is the impressive temple-shaped memorial to Maharaja Ajit Singh. The Hall of Heroes has fifteen giant statues carved into the rock face of the mountain, depicting the local heroes and Hindu divinities.

The Clock tower is the heart of the old bazaar and retains its medieval charm. It is interesting to browse through the stalls selling spices, vegetables, colourful *odhnis* (scarves) and if you have the time you can get yourself Jodhpurs (typical riding trousers) stitched which have made this city famous in the international polo circuit.

Polo has been the favorite sport of Jodhpur with legendary Sir P and Rao Raja Hanut Singh dazzling the international circuit with their incredible flair. Sir P was twice the regent of Jodhpur. He was very popular with the British royalty. The emperor was known to consult him on vital issues. It was during his regency, that the Prince of Wales visited Jodhpur. The diamond "*sarpeech*" presented by him to the Queen Empress became her favourite piece of jewellery. In the First World War he led Jodhpur Lancers from the front. In the war, the lancers impressed everybody by their heroic bravery. It was in Jodhpur that Lord Mountbatten played his first "*chuckker*" of polo. Shivraj the young prince of the city is living up to the tradition of the game. The Raisana hill, in New Delhi, was in the village given as *Jagir* to the Rathores by the Mughals. Later it became the Viceroy's Palace, now it is the Rashtrapati Bhavan or the President's Palace.

Maharaja Gaj Singh, the thirty eighth ruler of forty clans of Rathores was only in his early twenties, when privy purses were taken away from the princes. It was not the losing of privileges that bothered him; it was the plight of the common citizen without any connections with the high places or resources that upset him more.

Today Jodhpur has developed into an important base for the armed forces. It also has the high court bench of the state of Rajasthan. Lately the artifacts produced at the numerous antique-producing factories are in great demand all over the world.

The neighbouring villages of Jodhpur are not to be outdone, especially Salawas, which has become the centre of cotton and camel wool kelims. The jeep safaris have become popular too, an ideal way to see the life of rural tribes, notably are the Bisnois. Their social structure is based on twenty nine commandments out of which protecting the trees and wildlife are the topmost. It is quite common to see Black buck, Chinkara deer, and Damosile crane roaming around without any fear of harm in their villages. An hour's drive takes one to the temple town of Osian. A rich trading centre of the past, it is famous for its Hindu and Jain temples.

Jodhpur is the gateway to the Thar Desert, and to the city of Jaisalmer. Spending the night on the sand dunes on the way to Jaisalmer is an incredible experience.

JAISALMER

Approaching the city by road, after miles and miles of arid expanse of land, Jaisalmer rises out of the desert like a mirage. Once the capital of Bhatti Rajputs, it was

Camel driver getting ready for the day after spending the night at the Pushkar fair

founded by Rao Jaisal in the year 1157. Throughout history it faced threats from the Mughals and the neighbouring Rajputs alike. In the fourteenth century the invading Muslim armies laid a siege for seven months forcing all the womenfolk to commit *Juhar*, or self-immolation while the men raced out of the city gates with the shrouds as their headgear to face certain death.

This western outpost of India somehow has managed to retain its fairytale atmosphere down the centuries. A walk through the cobble street lanes transports one down centuries. The brightly painted doors, windows, and richly caved facades of the houses set a picturesque contrast with the blue sky of the desert. Almost 5000 people live inside the fort along with cows and goats, which are totally at home in its narrow streets. The fort itself is surrounded by 40 feet high curvilinear walls that date back to the seventeenth century. The four gates of the fort date about a century earlier. Inside the gates, which are also known as *pols*, the local musicians along with their dancing children welcome the visitors.

The winding lane takes one to the main plaza or *chowk* where the king reviewed his troops and received petitions. The marble throne along the entrance of the palace was used in the *Rajtilak* or the coronation ceremonies. The palace itself is quite insipid compared to the other palaces of Rajasthan. There are some incredible carvings of the *jharokas* or balconies, which appear as if they are made of wood. From the roof of this five- storey palace one can have the panoramic view of the fort and the surrounding areas. On the top of the roof is a giant metallic umbrella, which is the standard of the royal family.

Another important landmark within the fort is the group of Jain temples. Although the Bhatti Rajputs are Hindus, the Jains were accepted in their fold. The temples are richly adorned with carved pillars, arches and cupolas. The images of the Jain Prophets are in white marble, black marble and in the alloy of the five metals. In the morning temples are active with worshippers performing puja and the temples are filled with the aroma of saffron and sandalwood. Inside the main temple there is the treasure room, which has some old manuscripts and images of the prophet in precious metals and stones.

Outside the fort walls the bazaar is equally interesting. The villagers throng it from the surrounding area in their colourful attire and jewellery. They can be seen crowding in the silversmith store or getting their clothes stitched at the tailor's shop. There are numerous shops that now cater to western tourists. One can look for inexpensive clothes, camel leather shoes, silver jewellery and cheap restaurants.

Off the main streets, in the by-lanes of the city, are scattered treasure trove of *havelis*, the merchant houses. These are carved out of the local golden sandstone and every inch is decorated with incredible carvings. The most noteworthy are Patwon-ki-Haveli, built for five brothers; these are five buildings adjacent to each other with different facades.

The city merchants made lot of money as tradesmen since Jaisalmer was lying on the trade routes from the central Asia to the coast in the Sindh region. The merchandise was carried by the caravans of camels. Opening up of the sea routes proved to be the death knell for these trade routes. In 1947 when the country was divided into India and Pakistan the trade came to a standstill. A boon in disguise for the city proved to be the wars with Pakistan. Its location close to the border made it into a big army and air force base. Along came the infrastructure like roads and the railways. In 1973 two French journalists wrote about the city for French newspapers and since then the city has not looked back. Initially it was the French tourists who visited the city; nowadays visitors of every nationality can be seen in the city. The popularity of the destination is evident by the recent introduction of commercial flights in the tourist season.

From Jaisalmer the most popular excursion these days is the camel safari in the sand dunes of Sam and Khuri, which have gained popularity in the recent times.

The Indian movie director Satyajit Ray had rightly called it *Sonar Qila*, the golden fort. From the cenotaphs of the royalty, which are situated on the ridge across the city, the sunset is truly a moving experience. Louduvara near the city is a ghost village, which was abandoned overnight to save the honour of a village belle who refused the advances of a local chieftain.

BIKANER

Incensed by a comment of Rao Jodha (the founder of Jodhpur) made in the *Durbar*, Rao Bika left Jodhpur for good. On the way he was blessed by a female mystic, Karni Mata, who predicted that he would end up becoming more famous than his father. In the north of Rajasthan he carved out this desert state in 1488, which is roughly the size of England and named his new capital city, Bikaner. Being in the heart of the arid zone, there was not much agriculture activity, but it soon became a trading and financial outpost. It was on the route which the caravans took from Asia to the coast in western India. Later it became a camel producing centre and the breed is in great demand even today.

Although less aesthetically appealing than Jaisalmer, Bikaner is still an interesting place to visit. It boasts a spectacular fort and an old city dotted with *havelis* and surrounded by high crenellated walls.

Raja Rai Singh, a general in the army of the Mughal Emperor Akbar, constructed the Junagarh Fort, a landmark of the city, in late sixteenth century. Later rulers added palaces and temples in this fort. The fort is not as imposing as the forts in Jodhpur and Amber, which are perched on the hilltops. But the superbly sculpted palaces, temples and towers make a picturesque ensemble unrivalled in their magnificence. The location of the city in the heart of the harsh desert kept the attackers at bay. The local citizens are proud to point out that it has never been conquered.

Upon entering the main courtyard lies the Karan Mahal with gold leaf paintings on its pillars and walls. It was built to commemorate the victory over the Mughal Emperor Aurangzeb. The Phool Mahal or Flower Palace was built during the reign of Maharaja Gaj Singh. The main feature of this palace is a marble statue of *Surya*, the Sun God and the brightly painted walls and ceilings depicting scenes from the Ramayana. Anup Mahal is the grandest construction and was commissioned by Maharaja Karni Singh. It features wooden ceilings inlaid with mirror and delicate latticework on the windows and balconies. The Chandra Mahal is the most opulent room in the fort and is filled with treasures like precious- stone- encrusted paintings and statues of gilded deities.

The most recently constructed part of the fort is the Ganga Singh hall, which was built in 1937. It houses a museum exhibiting weapons used by the Bikaner Camel Crops also known as Ganga Risala.

High walls also surround the atmospheric old city of Bikaner and main attractions here are some extraordinary *havelis* and temples. The most impressive *havelis* are the Rampuria Haveli and the Bhanwar Niwas Haveli. Both of these are located at the heart of the old city and the latter is now a hotel.

The temples include the two Jain temples of Bhandreshwar and Sandeshwar. Both these temples were built by two Jain brothers and are stunning in their use of colour and intricate wall paintings, a rare feature in Rajasthan's Jain temples.

Rao Lunkaran built Laxminath Temple, which is a Hindu temple, in the sixteenth century. Laxminath was the patron god of the ruler of Bikaner and during major religious festivals, a royal procession led by the Maharaja paid homage at the temple.

Lal Garh Palace in the north of the town is the home to the royal family of Bikaner, although parts now serve as a hotel. Although it is an imposing building with overhanging balconies and delicate latticework, it certainly does not come close to the other beautiful royal residences of Rajasthan.

The Palace also houses Shri Sadul Museum that displays a collection of artifacts and personal possessions of the Bikaner maharajas. There are photographs of tiger shoots that was the most sought after sport of the early twentieth century. In front of the Palace is a carriage from the Maharaja's royal train; its wood panelled carriages and brass fitting are reminiscent of their opulent past in which the maharajas of India use to travel. Hundreds of servants would travel along with the royalty to make their stay more comfortable.

A little further off the main city is the Ganga Golden Jubilee Museum, which is fairly interesting and exhibits costumes, weapons, ornaments and ancient statues and paintings. A visit to the camel breeding farm just outside the town is recommended, where the experts answer all your queries, regarding this multipurpose animal of the desert.

Close to Bikaner in the village of Deshnok is the most curious temple dedicated to the local goddess Karni Mata. Thousands of holy rats are worshipped as they are recognized as the local bards who were turned into rats, when the Goddess Karni Mata wanted to prove a point to Yamaraj, the god of the dead. The pure silver doors of the temple and the marble carvings are truly fascinating.

Maharaja Ganga Singh could be easily called the father of modern Bikaner. His famous Bikaner Camel Crops won great laurels in China and Egypt. He brought Ganga canal for irrigation, which turned this arid region into fertile land. His grouse shoots were so famous that to be invited was a huge honour. The British Royal family and the Viceroy all shot duck at Gajner. Later the descendant of Ganga Singh, Maharaja Karni Singh followed the tradition by representing India in the Olympics in skeet shooting.

(Opposite page) Intricately carved door, inlaid with ivory, leading to the palace balcony of Bikaner

The Umaid Bhavan Palace is the last royal residence to be built in India. Maharaja Umaid Singh of Jodhpur commissioned it as a famine relief project for his citizens. The British architect Mr. Lanchshire conceived its design in 1948

(Opposite page) A fifteenth century audience hall in the majestic Meherangarh Fort of Jodhpur. The ceiling and the walls are richly decorated with gold and mineral colours while the floor is covered with rare Mughal carpets

Locals in their traditional turbans at the silversmiths shop in the bazaar of Jaisalmer
(Opposite page) A Rathore Rajput sitting outside his home painted in typical blue of Jodhpur. This colour is extensively used
in the Jodhpur city as it provides relief to the eyes in the harsh desert sun

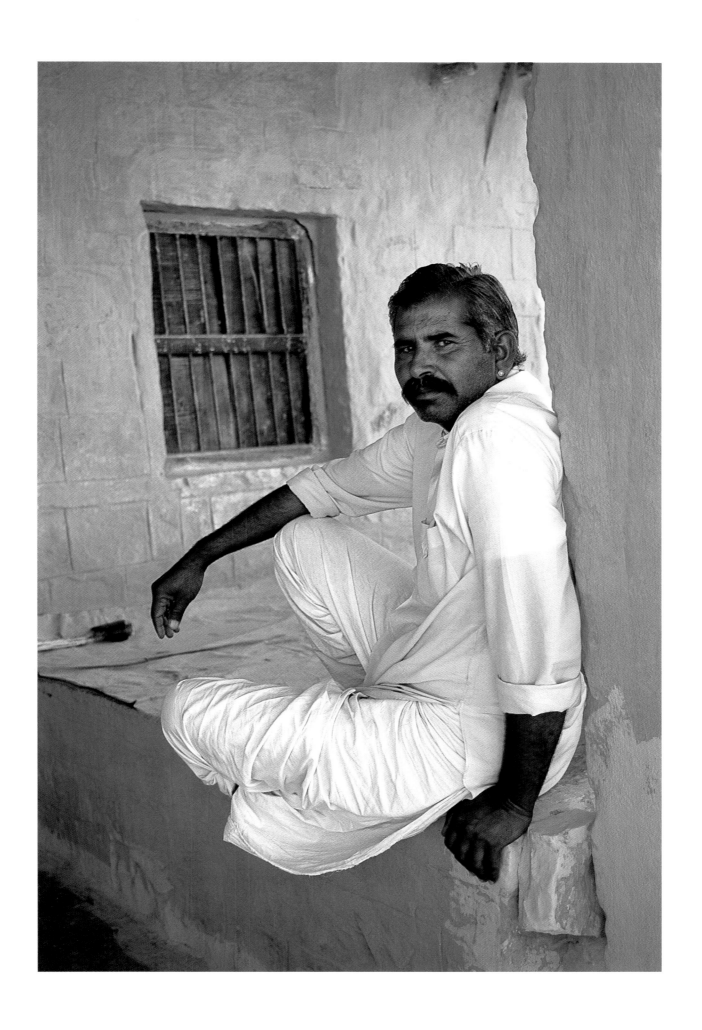

Inside view of a Jain temple in the town of Jaisalmer. The Jain community who have traditionally been traders, have contributed substantially to the town's economy

The golden coloured stone images of Jain prophets are the characteristic of the Jaisalmer region
(Opposite page) Richly carved interiors of the Jain temples inside the Jaisalmer Fort
(Following page) At sunset, camel drivers wait to take the visitors on the sand dunes of Thar Desert
(Page after following page) Richly carved façade in the golden sandstone of a merchant house or haveli, which dot the narrow streets of this town

Camel driver on his way home crosses the dry bed of river Jamuna. The golden light of dusk
adds to the romantic beauty of Taj Mahal

Dule Raja, the handsome warrior prince of the Kachhwaha clan of the Rajputs, founded the ancient capital Amber in 1128. For centuries this warrior caste protected the frontiers of the country. However, it was not until the twenty-second Maharaja, Raja Jai Singh, ascended the throne, six centuries later that he moved the capital to the present city of Jaipur. The old capital at Amber could not accommodate the growing number of people and besides the town had a severe water shortage.

safe for its inhabitants.

Jai Singh's fascination for science, mathematics and astronomy led him to build massive open-air observatories not only in the capital city but also in Delhi, Mathura, Ujjain and Varanasi. Besides telling the time, these complicated astronomical instruments calculated the height and position of heavenly bodies, read the altitude and distances in the sky and tell both the time and the sun's path in the heavens. A thirty-meter-high sundial that indicated the hour when the sun's shadow moved every

JAIPUR, DELHI, AGRA

Raja Jai Singh planned the city, as we know it today. He enlisted the help of his chief architect Vidhyadhar from Bengal and separated the city into nine blocks, which were further divided into 107 sub-blocks in what was perhaps the first attempt at urban planning in India.

The Maharaja personally supervised the plans of this new city, which he named after himself. The principles of the *Shilpa Shastra*, an ancient architectural treatise, were incorporated in the plans and the result was a beautifully symmetrical city that was both aesthetic and

four meters, to gauge the time of day. Another achievement was an instrument that measured planetary and astral positions in the universe.

Jaipur is also known as the Pink City because in 1876, the entire city was painted pink, symbolic of hospitality, to welcome the Prince of Wales who never showed up.

Maharaja Pratap Singh built Jaipur's signature building, the *Hawa Mahal* or Palace of Winds, in 1799. Located in the centre of the town, it has a pink sandstone façade, and is five storeys high but only one room deep.

Hawa Mahal was the discreet vantage point from where the ladies in *purdah*, peering through the honeycombed windows, could watch the action below.

The City Palace is the official residence of the Maharajas of Jaipur. It was partly converted into a museum in 1959 and houses many royal treasures. One of the two main objects of interest is the two-meter-wide pajamas and two and a half-meter-long tunic that once clothed Raja Madho Singh, a heavy man of two hundred and fifty kilograms.

The other major attraction is the Diwan-i-Khas in which are exhibited huge silver jars, each 350 kilograms in weight — the largest in the world. There is an interesting story about them that speaks of the religious sentiments of nineteenth and early twentieth century Hindu maharajas.

When the Maharaja was invited to the coronation of King Edward VII, a luxury liner was chartered and outfitted to suit his royal tastes. As a measure against stepping on impure, alien land on his arrival, sand from Jaipur was put inside his shoes and the silver jars were filled with the holy waters of the Ganges so that the Maharaja could purify himself at all times. Also, silver and gold offerings were made to the sea to ward off evil spirits. The silver jars, therefore, symbolized the King's compromise that enabled him to travel overseas and yet remain pure.

The nearby Diwan-i-am contains beautiful collection of illustrated manuscripts and fabulous carpets, including world's only *pashmina* wool carpet that once adorned the palace walls and floors. The present Maharaja, 'Bubbles' to his friends, resides with his family in their private apartments in Chandra Mahal.

The Rambagh Palace, the other royal palace outside the city wall was built as the hunting lodge of Maharaja Ram Singh, in the eighteenth century. It was later converted into a royal guesthouse. Raja Madho Singh II, who had then ascended the throne, instructed Sir Jacob Swinton, a British resident architect, to refurbish it. Maharaja Sawai Man Singh II- 'Jai' — decided to make it his residence in the 1930s. He lived here with his three wives; his third wife, Maharani Gayatri Devi, beautiful princess of Coochbehar, was just thirteen years old when they fell in love. They were married in 1940. After he died in England in 1970 during a polo game, the Maharani then moved to the Lily Pool behind the palace, where she still lives. Today Rambagh Palace is a luxury hotel and boasts of exotic suites, a fabulous dining hall and the best bar in India, the original Polo Bar.

The Amber Palace, eleven kilometers north of Jaipur, comes into view around the last bend in the winding road. Built by Mughal artisans during the reign of Man Singh I in the sixteenth century, the palace is set amid the charming Aravali hills. It boasts of paintings and marble panels set in relief by artists of the Mughal court. Of particular beauty is the art of mirror inlay-work in wet plaster,

which would reflect a thousand stars against the ceiling even if a single flame was lit in the room.

A leisurely ride up to the fort by elephant offers a panoramic view of the city and its majestic walls with guard towers. It is an unforgettable experience for any visitor.

Within the palace is the Kali Mata Temple. The image of the goddess, the manifestation of divine energy, was brought from Jessor in Bengal and installed here by Maharaja Man Singh I in 1604. The temple is made of white marble, which is exquisitely carved by the local artisans. The entrance door is made out of silver and depicts the Goddess Kali in her many forms of feminine energy. Above the door is a statue of Lord Ganesha carved out of a single piece of coral.

Within walking distance of Amber lies the Jaigarh Fort, which was the treasury of the Kachhwaha clan. Tales of a hidden royal treasure still do the rounds among the local people. It houses the biggest cannon in the country, though not a single shot has ever been fired from it to date.

Jaipur is well known for its colourful bazaars, which their founder, Jai Singh, had planned. He wanted the city to be recognized for its elaborate artistry and fine craftsmanship. His wish is alive today in the dazzling array of precious stones jewellery, brassware, carpets, miniature paintings and antiques that can be found in various parts of the city.

DELHI

It is often said that the history of India is the history of Delhi. New Delhi, the capital of India, has always occupied a strategic position in the country's history as different Hindus and Islamic dynasties have ruled from here, leaving their imprint in the form of relics, which recapture those bygone times. Its history goes back to the days of the Mahabharata when the *Pandavas* lived on the banks of the river Yamuna. Their kingdom, near Indraprastha, has been identified as Delhi. Indraprastha later became Dhillika, the first of the seven medieval cities of Delhi. Its significant location, about 1,000 kilometers from the Khyber Pass (the entrance point for most foreign invaders) increased its importance as a vital strategic position in the defence of the country.

Qila Rai Pithora, the first known city of Prithviraj Chauhan III, was taken over by Mohammed Ghori. Qutub-ud-Din Aibak, who succeeded him to the throne after his death, made Delhi his capital in 1192. As these foreigners made the newly conquered lands their home, they gradually began to incorporate the Indian way in their lifestyles, thereby evolving a whole new culture. These influences are most evident in Indo-Islamic architecture, which reflects the cultural synthesis that has taken place in Delhi over the centuries. An example of this unique style is found in the Quwat-ul-Islam mosque, where the Islamic style arches and calligraphy is beautifully blended

with floral designs. In marked contrast, the columns of the mosque are of destroyed Hindu and Jain temples.

The Khalji Sultanate, which came to power in 1290 after toppling the Sultans, raised the second Delhi township of Siri, northeast of the Qila Rai Pithora. The Tughluqs, who ruled after the Khaljis, built the third city of Tughluqabad to the extreme south of Delhi; and then the cities of Jahanpanah and Kotla Firoz Shah on the banks of the river Yamuna. When the Mughals replaced the Lodhi dynasty in the early sixteenth century, its founder, Babur, concentrated on developing Agra and made it his capital. But his son, Humayun, constructed a new capital on the banks of the river Yamuna around the ancient capital and called it Din Panah. He also built a citadel, the Purana Qila. Shah Jahan, successor to Jahangir, created Shahjahanabad along the river as the well planned, seventh township of Delhi. It remained the Mughal capital until 1857, despite the decline of the Mughal Empire since 1707.

In 1857, when the British Crown took over the running of India from the East India Company, the viceroy and the government were at Calcutta, the commercial capital because of its access to the tea gardens and coal fields. However, in 1911, the decision was made to establish a new capital at Delhi, which was more centrally located. Plans were made to build a new city to befit the 'Jewel in the British Crown'. The area along the ridge, south of Shahjahanabad, was chosen as the site for the imperial capital. It was built on a regal scale by January 1931. Though the city has grown enormously after Independence in 1947, it is this area that boasts many of the best landmarks bequeathed by the British.

Lutyens and Baker designed much of the red sandstone architecture along the stretch between India Gate at one end and Rastrapathi Bhawan (the President's residence) at the other, with the adjoining administrative buildings of North Block and South Block, Parliament House and Connaught Place nearby. A number of other equally imposing complexes have come up on this area, which is still the administrative and commercial centre of the city.

For all its imposing presence, twentieth century British architecture pales in significance when compared with the relics of dynasties gone before.

The Rock Edict of the Buddhist emperor Ashoka (273-236 B.C.) in south Delhi, the best known of pre-Islamic relics, bears the inscription of the great emperor's appeal to follow the path of peace and righteousness. A similar call to the people is expressed in the writings on two pillars, one that is located in the ruins of Kotla Firoz Shah, whilst the other stands in close proximity to the renowned University of Delhi.

Perhaps the most famous among the Islamic relics is the Qutub Minar. Begun in 1199 by Sultan Qutub-ub-Din Aibak as a minaret to call the faithful to prayer, it served as a victory memorial as well. In recent times it has been closed to the general public as the tower became the preferred suicide spot for jilted lovers. In 1311, Ala-ud-Din Khalji added the Alai Darwaza, which allows entry to the southern end of the Qutub Minar enclosure. The elaborate tomb of Iltutmish, which stands within the same compound, is a classical example of early Islamic architecture. Further south lies the abandoned township of Tughluqabad, one of the seven cities of Delhi, which was developed with an emphasis on town planning and defense. A citadel and a reservoir still remain, stark reminders of a once glorious era.

Well laid-out gardens and beautiful mausoleums are among the more enduring achievements of Islamic rule in Delhi. The area north of Tughluqabad is littered with tombstones, some of which date back to the thirteenth century. The most well known among them is the tomb built in memory of the *Sufi* saint, Nizam-ud-Din Chisti, who died in 1325. The tomb acquired the status of a shrine over the years, and today thousands of devotees come here to pray and ask for the fulfilment of their wishes. Humayun's tomb, on which the Taj Mahal was later modelled, is to the east of the Nizam-ud-Din's shrine, while the Purana Qila-or Old Fort-is to the north and encloses a mosque and the sixteenth- century Sher Mandal, a two-storied octagonal pavilion.

Within the beautiful Lodi Gardens to the west are some tombs and mosques from the various Muslim dynasties, which established themselves prior to the Mughals. Safdarjung's Tomb of an early eighteenth century noble, near the Lodi Gardens, is equally well preserved. The need to surround their mausoleums with flowers was a constant feature of Muslim design which has been preserved by the Archaeological Survey of India despite the spread of urbanization.

While the mausoleums and monuments, forts and arches speak of the grandeur of Indo-Islamic rule, none match the eloquent style of the Red Fort, which is situated on the bank of the river Yamuna beside the Jama Masjid, the chief mosque of the Muslims in India.

Red Fort or Quila Mubarak as it was originally called was planned as the residence and office of Emperor Shah Jahan. It was later used by the British as an army cantonment and armoury. The Fort was developed as a self-contained unit. The meticulous planning and detail, especially with regard to defence against an enemy, beside the fine expression of Mughal art, make a visit there mandatory. A moat surrounds the fort and was once filled by the Yamuna until the river changed its course — an almost painful reminder of the decline of the all-powerful Mughals.

The Red Fort overlooks Chandni Chowk (Silver

Holy books in Jama Masjid, the Friday mosque in Delhi
(Following page) Minaret of the tomb Itmad-ud-Daulah at Agra

Square), an old market crisscrossed by a labyrinth of by-lanes and renowned for its sweetmeats, crafts and traditional - especially silver - jewellery. The canal that divided the main thoroughfare once flowed with the waters of the river Yamuna. Along the main street, a dilapidated church still remains, the only remnant of a bygone era that has survived the passage of time. The fountain at watchtower that once stood beside it was pulled down in the 1950s to facilitate the flow of traffic and to accommodate urban growth and development.

To the north of the Red Fort is Metcalfe House, built in 1835 to house the British resident, and St. James Church, built in 1824. Civil Lines is the stretch between the church and the University of Delhi in the north, and is filled with relics of the Raj and the earlier Mughal rule. The tombs, gardens and mosques, well over a hundred years old, stand as ample evidence of Delhi's varied past.

AGRA

Agra has as much historic importance as Delhi. When the great Mughal emperor, Akbar, made Agra his capital in 1556, it became India's most important city. He was very impressed with the commanding position of an old fort called Badalgarh, high on the banks of the Yamuna River, and decided to make it his capital. The twenty-meter high outer walls of the Agra Fort, two and a half kilometers in circumference, and the river were an almost impregnable line of defence. These features encouraged Akbar to make up his mind about establishing his centre of control here. The fort was a township in itself. The members of the royal family and their entourage were housed in palaces and other buildings along the river, including the Jasmine Tower, where Emperor Shah Jahan was imprisoned before his death. The Diwan-e-Am (hall of public audience) used to be decorated with carpets and curtains woven with gold and silver threads while the royal suites had walls inlaid with precious stones and jewels. The royal family was never without entertainment, and animal fights in particular, below its ramparts were a source of much amusement.

In the vicinity of the Agra Fort, stands the world's most photographed monument—the Taj Mahal. It is a mausoleum built during the reign of Shah Jahan for his wife, Mumtaz Mahal, who died in 1630. The story of their first meeting is as romantic as the Taj itself. It is said that he met her at the Mina Bazaar, held every Friday, where the wives and daughters of nobility sold artefacts to the male members of the royal house. On one occasion, Shah Jahan went to the bazaar and enquired of the lady at the *mishery* (sugar candy) stall the price of a piece of candy. She quoted the price of a large diamond in jest, but the emperor paid the huge

price demanded. The woman started laughing at the emperor for having mistaken the candy for a diamond and lifted the veil from her face. Shah Jahan caught a glimpse of her beauty and vowed to marry her even though he was already married. Their romance was a long and happy one with Mumtaz never leaving his side until she died giving birth to her fourteenth child.

Taj Mahal, 'dream in marble', was built to honour Mumtaz's dying wish for a memorial to their love. It took twenty-two years and twenty thousand workers helped to create this masterpiece. Its perfection and beauty would not have been possible without the deft planning of Ustad Ahmad Lahori and Isa Khan, master architects of the Mughal court, who designed the symmetry and proportion and every detail of the fine calligraphic and pietra dura ornamentation. The entire complex includes the forecourt and lofty entrance, a Mughal garden with canals, a central tank with a series of fountains, and the tomb proper, flanked by a mosque to its west and a guest house to the east. The graves are in an underground crypt and are encased in marble delicately decorated with semiprecious stones. The emperor had planned a similar tomb for himself, in black marble, on the oppsite bank of the river Jamuna. In his later years his son imprisoned him. Finally he was buried beside his beloved.

Itmad-ud-Daulah is another exquisite marble tomb in Agra. Its beauty is unfairly eclipsed by the fame and size of the Taj. It is lavishly decorated with *pietra dura* floral and geometric design. This gives the building a delicate appearance when viewed from a distance. The tomb is dedicated to Mirza Ghiyas Beg, a Persian noble and his wife. Their beautiful daughter Mehrunissa eventually became the empress Nur Jahan. This helped Mirza to climb the ranks of the noblemen and was given the title of Itmad-ud-Daulah, or the pillar of the state.

The tomb was built in 1628. It was the first bold expression in white marble structure situated in a *charbag* (four garden) and completely decorated with *pietra dura*. It is often described as the 'baby Taj', and looks like a jewel box from the entrance gate.

FATEHPUR SIKRI

About fifty kilometers south of Agra is the ghost town of Fatehpur Sikri. Built entirely of locally quarried red sand stone, it is a splendid accomplishment of design and architecture of medieval India. Its dramatic location on top of the ridge, in barren landscape, adds to its imperial status.

The reason for the imperial city to be built so close to the already existing Mughal capital, Agra is credited to Sheikh Salim Chisti, a *Sufi* saint who predicted the birth of Akbar's male heir. Others point it out to be a calculated political move by Akbar, to uproot the nobility and keep them under check at a newer location. In some ways it could be compared to the shifting of the capital to Versailles by Louise the XV.

The building of Fatehpur Sikri was a creative expression of extraordinary scale in medieval India. It was built within a span of fourteen years as the new capital of the Mughal Empire. Some 8000 workers worked on the site creating a beautiful lake on the edge of the city. The cost of construction is estimated at two million rupees. One rupee in those days was made up of 96% pure silver and weighed 178 grams.

After a short stay of fourteen years, Akbar marched out with his army in 1585 to control the Afghan rebellion. He positioned himself at Lahore closer to the Northwest border. After taking care of the problem, Akbar returned to Agra and never went back to inhabit Fatehpur Sikri. The city was thus abandoned; many parts of the city have somehow survived the ravages of time.

The city was built on a grid pattern with the buildings aligning from east to west in north-south axis. The buildings at Fatehpur Sikri can be divided into three types. Public congregational buildings like the Jama Masjid and Diwan-i-am. Semi-official areas such as Diwan-i-khas, Anup Talao and private enclosures such as Jodhabai's Palace and Begum Mariyam's Palace. The local stonecutters worked with the artisans from Rajasthan and Gujarat. The latter translated Gujarati woodwork designs into that of red sandstone. Some other buildings were copies of Mughal camp tents. The architecture of the city is spectacular, especially its vaulted ceilings, which are supported by stone slabs acting as ribs. The majority of the structures use post and beam design with *duchhati* (two floors) and *tibra* (three arch) elements. Some of the architectural wonders of Fatehpur Sikri are the Buland Darwaza, the giant gateway to Jama Masjid. Unique Diwan-i-khas or Ekstambha Prasada, popularly known as the hall of private audience, was probably a replica of a bird roost of Gujarat. It may have been used by Akbar to review state jewels.

The city is vividly described in the accounts of western travellers such as Catalan Padre Antonio Monserrat and English traveller Ralph Finch. Court historians Abu'l Fazl and Badauni have also left detailed accounts of the everyday life of the palace and its citizens. Originally the main entrance of the city was from the lakeside. There were two stone elephants flanking this ceremonial entrance and was thus called, Hathi Pol. Heeran Minar (elephant tower) in front of Hathi pol was probably a light house (*akash deep*) to guide travellers to the main entrance of the city.

The religious tolerance of Akbar gave boost to the creativity in the new capital. Thousands of artisans worked in the court to produce illustrated manuscripts, calligraphy, gold seals, carpets and tapestry. Religious debates were encouraged; Ibadat Khana was used for such purpose. *Jizyah*, tax on non-Muslims was removed. Solar calendar was adopted. Hindu epics were translated from Sanskrit to Persian. In order to have good relations with neighbouring Rajputs, Akbar married Jodhabai, the princesses from Amber. *Din-i-Ilahi* was declared as state religion which respected all religions equally. These reforms struck a chord with the Hindu majority who were ruled by the Muslim minority. The Indianization of the Mughal dynasty was initiated.

The opulence of the Mughal court is not hard to imagine. It is said that at sunset, Anup Talao, the water tank in front of emperor's palace, was filled with perfumed water. Floating lamps would illuminate the tank, the court musician Tansen, seated in the central platform of the tank, would weave magic with his evening *ragas*. The only other sound filling the evening air would emanate from the *ghungroo* (ankle bells) of the nauch girls. It would appear as if the stars had descended from the heaven into Anup Talao. Ralph Finch notes that Fatepore or Fatehpur Sikri was much greater and more populous than London.

The white marble tomb of the Sufi saint, Sheikh Salim Chisti is located in the north of the courtyard of the mosque, Jama Masjid. It was the first elaborate marble structure in the Mughal empire. The tomb has some exquisite carvings in its marble screens and columns. A mother of pearl canopy covers the grave of the saint. Following the centuries old tradition, hundreds of devotees make a pilgrimage here to offer prayers and tie threads in the lattice windows of the saint's grave in order to have their wishes come true- just the way the Mughal emperor Akbar did some 430 years ago.

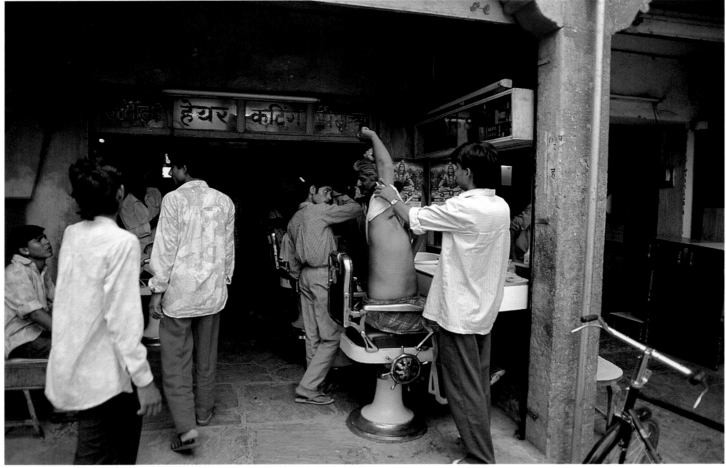

Streets in India are full of life, here in Jaipur one can see various activities in progress (Opposite page top) Piyau, or charity water stall quenching thirst of the passerby (Opposite page below) Nai or barber at work in his saloon (Above) Dudhwala or milkman distributing milk on his bike (Previous pages) Bronze doors of the City Palace in Jaipur flanking the ceremonial elephant headgear (Pages 126-127) Amer Palace and fort reflecting the waters of the lake at sunrise

Elephant with full makeup and decked in finery on the occasion of the Teej festival in Jaipur.
Colourful crowds from the neighbouring villages turn out in large numbers to witness such events

The Albert Hall in Ram Niwas Garden was designed by Sir S. Swinton Jacob in Indo-Saracenic style. It is one of many such buildings that was designed by European architects using local elements
(Opposite page) The prominent landmark of the Pink City Jaipur is the honey combed Hawa Mahal or the Palace of the winds. It was made for the ladies of the royalty to see the processions in the street below
(Following Page) Local woman waiting under the nineteenth century frescoes executed on the havelis of wealthy Marwari merchants in Shekhawati region of Rajasthan, making the entire region a living museum

Richly decorated hall of private audience in Samodhe Palace near Jaipur shows the opulence of the days gone by
(Previous page) When the power of the Mughals' faded, the court artisans found new patrons among the various maharajas of Rajasthan,
where they decorated the palace walls with Mughal motifs as seen in the palaces of Amer and Jaipur
(Following page) Local women dressed in their festive clothes waiting to accompany the Teej procession in Jaipur

(Above) Red Fort of Delhi as seen from the Chandni Chowk, the main street of old Delhi. The fort was the seat of Mughal empire since the seventeenth century. In 1857 the British occupied it and exiled the last Mughal emperor Bahadur Shah Zafar to Rangoon, in Burma (Below) Hall of public audience or Diwan-i Am, has beautifully engraved marble throne in the centre where the emperor would sit listening to the state matters (Opposite page) Domes of Jama Masjid and Old Delhi in the background as seen from the towering minaret of the mosque (Previous page) Qutab Minar is Delhi's oldest (1199) and most well preserved monument. Nearby is the marble grave of Iltutmish with richly carved mirab on the western wall. He is attributed with the last four storeys of his father-in-law's incredible minaret

(Previous page) View of the Taj Mahal as seen from the top of the entrance gate at sunrise, the central pool and the four garden (charbag) design are clearly visible. Pietra dura design decorate the marble palaces in the Jasmine Tower of the Agra Fort

*(Top) View of the tomb of Itmad-ud-Daulah colloquially called the Baby Taj, the entire marble façade of the tomb
is inlaid with colourful designs of semi -precious stones
(Opposite page) Faithful gather in the mosque of Taj Mahal on the occasion of the Muslim festival of Id*

(Previous page) View of the veranda circumnavigating the tomb of Sheikh Salim Chisti in Fatehpur Sikri.
The sixteenth century tomb is thronged by the pilgrims desiring a child. Its perforated marble screens are of utmost magnificence

View of the mosque which houses the tomb of the Sufi saint Sheikh Salim Chishti. The saint prophesied the birth of an heir to Emperor Akbar
(Top) View of the ghost city of Fatehpur Sikri made entirely of locally quarried red sand stone.

The river front of Benares or Varanasi mesmerizes the visitor with cacophony of sounds, sights and smell.
This morning view of the boat ride on the Ganges river remains etched in the memory of the visitor for the rest of his conscious life
(Following page) Sculpture of apsara or the celestial dancer playing the flute in Laxmana temple Khajuraho
(Page after following page) The entire surface of these tenth century temples of Khajuraho is covered with the sculptures of gods,
goddesses, celestial nymphs, erotic couples, soldiers and animals. On the left is the world famous frieze of the
Kandharia Mahadev temple. Right the view of the Jain temple from the eastern group with its soaring shikhar at Khajuraho

The temples of Khajuraho are the manifestation of cultural synthesis and creative energy that once dominated medieval India. They are located in Khajuraho, in the central Indian State of Madhya Pradesh, and are the best-preserved medieval temples of India. The temples are built from buff-coloured sandstone mined from the diamond quarries of Panna, situated on the east bank of the river Ken. The temples are dedicated to Savia, Vashnavia and Jaina sects, and inspite of divergent sectarian affiliations, the dominant architectural and sculptural schemes are uniformly

were constructed in the tenth century by the Chandela dynasty, who made Khajuraho their religious capital. Later they were deserted with the advent of Islam. The site lay in disuse and was forgotten for eight centuries until 1838, when a British engineer rediscovered them. Their restoration took place through the patronage of the kings of nearby Chattarpur and Panna. Today they are one of the heritage sites of the world.

The statues of gods and goddesses, warriors, celestial dancers or *apsaras* and animals adorn different levels of

KHAJURAHO, VARANASI, SARNATH

homogeneous. The difference lies basically in the presiding deity of each temple. The temples mark the culmination of the central Indian style, which is recognized with lofty *shikhars*, high platforms and no enclosures. All temples are built on the axis of east-to-west and are divided into four major parts: the *ardhmandapa* (entrance porch), the *mandapa* (hall), *antrala* (vestibule) and *garbha-griha* (sanctum sanctorum) all are inter-connected by a common passage.

There used to be eighty-five temples in all, but today only twenty-two survive. These central Indian style temples

temple façade and are exceedingly elaborate. The sculptures of *apsaras*, the heavenly dancers, sensitively portray the sensuous movements of their bodies with provocative undertones. The erotic sets of sculptures of couples in every conceivable sexual position are called *mithuna*. They represent the transition from the physical to the spiritual plane of the individual. Their life-like exuberance has been the focus of attraction down the ages. Some of the postures depicted are so complicated that they are possible only with the assistance of attendants.

The pursuance of *Kama* (physical pleasure) was one of the four aims of life according to Vatsayana, the author of Kama Sutra. The Hindu philosophy of *Yoga* (spiritual exercise) and *Bhoga* (physical pleasure), the two paths that lead to *Moksha* (final liberation) is the underlying theme of these sculptures.

The best-preserved temple with its four subsidiary shrines is the Lakshmana Temple dedicated to Vishnu, the lord of preservation. A candle kept aflame at the back of the main idol gives a celestial aura. It is a treat to watch it at dawn when the sun's rays first kiss Lord Vishnu's feet before lighting up the whole statue.

The tallest temple, the Kandariya Mahadev is dedicated to Lord Shiva and has a *Shikhara* (spire), which is thirty-eight meters high. Of its many statues, the most interesting is the one of a yogi performing the *shirsh asana* (headstand while having intercourse with three women at the same time). The statues are a window to the Indian concept of feminine beauty - large eyes, big breasts and swelling hips.

The best time in the year to visit Khajuraho is March when the leading dancers of the country perform against the backdrop of the Kandariya Mahadev Temple, in a replay of what must have happened centuries ago when devdasis, the temple dancers used to entertain the gods.

VARANASI

"Older than history, older than tradition, older even than legend, and looks twice as old as all of them put together, that is Benares". Mark Twain

Varanasi, or *Kashi* (City of Light), is an ancient town situated on the left bank of the Ganges in Uttar Pradesh. It is one of the seven most sacred cities of Hinduism and legend has it that it rests on Lord Shiva's trident, a spiritual manifestation of the Lord of All. This holy town dates back to the first millennium BC. Varanasi derives its name from the two streams called Varuna and Assi. The city is also known as Benaras, which is a corrupted form of Varanasi.

Varanasi has been an important seat of learning and culture since time immemorial, and has attracted scholars and philosophers from every corner of India including Shankara, who laid the foundations of modern Hinduism; Patanjali, the Sanskrit grammarian; Ramanuja, the theologian and Mahavira and Buddha, the great religious reformers. It is the aspiration of every devout Hindu to go on a pilgrimage at least once in his lifetime and Varanasi is said to combine all the virtues of all other places of pilgrimage. It is therefore not surprising that each year well over a million pilgrims visit it. Varanasi has maintained its religious life since the sixth century BC in one continuous tradition and stands at the centre of the Hindu universe. All devout Hindus wish to die in Kashi as it is said to ensure Moksha or deliverance from the cycle of birth and rebirth.

Life and death go hand in hand in Varanasi. The Panch Kosi road holds special significance as anyone dying within the area has a sure passport to heaven. As it is not possible

for the vast multitude desiring salvation to move to the city, most expect at least to be cremated here or have their ashes scattered in the holy Ganga.

Cremation takes place all through the night and day. The chief priest of the cremation ground is known as *Raja Dom*. The earth of the Manikaran Ghat, which is the busiest crematorium, is said to be permanently hot.

The Ghats or flights of stone steps descending into the Ganges remain the single major attraction of this ancient city. The Brahmins wait for the pilgrims under huge straw parasols and help them in their ablutions for a small fee. The Varanasi waterfront is constantly milling with thousands of pilgrims from all over India coming for their ritual ablutions. At dawn thousands of pilgrims can be seen bathing in the river and symbolically washing away their sins.

The main temples in this ancient town that abound with holy places are the Vishwanath Temple, Durga Kund, Annapurna and Kal Bhairava. The existing temples date back to the recent past as the Muslim invaders destroyed the architecture of ancient and medieval Varanasi, with all its temples.

Apart from its temples Kashi is also famous for lovely silk brocades. Vanarasi saris are of intricate and colourful weaves that most Indian women include in their wedding trousseaux. Its paan, a betel leaf enclosing a mixture of areca nut, cardamom and lime, which Indians chew habitually, is also well known. A special variety of mango is also much sought after.

SARNATH

Sarnath is a sacred Buddhist centre for pilgrimage. It was here that Gautam Buddha delivered his first sermon after attaining enlightenment in Bodh Gaya. Also it was here he expounded the theory of "four noble truths". In Buddhist texts this incident is referred to as Darmachakra-paravartna or "turning the wheel of law". At Sarnath, Buddha laid the foundation of Sangha, the order of monks. The place where Buddha lived is now a temple called Mulagandhakuti Vihara. The temple is of great importance as it enshrines relics of Buddha. The walls of the temple are adorned with frescoes of the artist Kosetsu Nosu, depicting the important incidents of Buddha's life. Near the temple is the sapling of Bodhi tree under which Buddha attained enligtenment.

At the height of its glory there was a twenty-one-and-a-half meter tall statue of Buddha and a monastery that housed fifteen hundred monks. Though repeated Muslim invasions ruined many of the structures that represented the Buddhist influence of the time, the capital of Ashoka pillar, some beautiful statues of Buddha and the Dhamekh Stupa are still intact. The local archaeological museum, which has recovered specimens that stretch across a period of 1500 years, houses a seated Buddha of the sixth century and Ashoka's lion capital belonging to the third century B.C. The latter has been adopted as the national emblem of the country.

(Previous page) View of the old city of Varanasi with Alamgir Mosque dominating the skyline as seen from the Scindhia ghat
(Page before previous page) Two friezes from the medieval temples of the Chandela dynasty in Khajuraho reflect the fine craftsmanship of the artisan. The kama or love making panel below reflects the pleasures of the liberal society while the panel above depicts the the Guru giving a dance lesson

People from all over the country come to bathe in the holy waters of the river hence purifying their souls
(Opposite page) The ghats or the steps leading down to the river Ganges in Varanasi are full of life from sunrise to the sunset

167

Calcutta, the imperial capital of the Raj, was founded in 1690 by Job Charnock.
It remained capital of the empire till 1911 when it was shifted to Delhi. The Victoria Memorial is the mute reminder of the city's colonial heritage.
Today Calcutta in this last bastion of Marxist who have ruled the state of Bengal since 1977
(Previous pages) Close to Varanasi is the Buddhist pilgrim centre of Sarnath. It here in 523 B.C. Gautam Buddha gave his first sermon
to his five disciples. The spot is marked by Dhamekh Stupa built by emperor Ashoka in 323 B.C. On the left a Tibetan monk is seen walking in
front of the gold leaf offerings on the Stupa. On the right page a monk from Sri Lanka can be seen emerging out of the Buddhist temple
Mulagandhakuti Vihar. The temple marks the spot where Buddha lived

Calcutta (Kolkotta) is India's second largest city and the capital of West Bengal. Like Bombay (Mumbai) and Madras (Chennai) its roots lie in the European expansion in the seventeenth century. It was the showpiece capital of the Raj and the greatest colonial city of the past.

An English merchant trader, Job Charnock, founded Calcutta in 1690. By the time the East India Company established its headquarters on the banks of the river Hooghly, the riverside was already dotted with European acquired trading rights and a number of villages around the Hooghly. The battle of Plassey in 1758 made the British masters of Bengal and Calcutta remained the centre of the East India Company, until the Company handed over control to the Crown in 1857.

The city of Calcutta has a tangible British past. The Raj has left an indelible mark on Calcutta with its large, sprawling, Victorian style buildings. Although a majority of these colonial buildings have decayed and are in neglect, many still survive in some form or the other. These

CALCUTTA, BHUBANESHWAR, PURI, KONARAK

trading companies. Besides the British there were the French, Danes, Dutch, Portuguese and the Greeks. The East India Company bought land around the village of Sulanuti and amalgamated two other villages of Kalikata and Govindpur and leased them from the Emperor Aurangzeb to form the town of Calcutta. Calcutta probably derives its name from Kalikutir or the house of Kali. It has now been renamed Kolkata.

With trading success came plans for further development. In subsequent years the East India Company include the Victoria Memorial, St. Paul's Cathedral and the Indian Museum, which is one of the largest museums in Asia. Of the many Raj institutions to have survived is the Race Course, the Polo ground and several exclusive gentlemen's clubs.

Calcutta prospered as the main centre of commerce and trade and the political capital of British India until 1911, when the capital was transferred to Delhi. The decline of Calcutta as an international port came with the opening of the Suez Canal in 1869, the emergence of

Bombay and the end of the Opium trade.

BHUBANESHWAR

Bhubaneshwar, the capital of ancient Kalinga houses some of India's finest medieval temples. In the seventh century, the Shailodbhavas made it their capital and this period saw mounting religious fervor along with wealth and power. This prosperity is most evident in the ambitious temple architecture of this period. Some seven thousand-sandstone temples are believed to have been constructed around the Bindusagar, a holy tank, between the seventh and the twelfth century. The Lingaraja temple, a creation of the Ganga dynasty, marks a culmination of this period in temple architecture. However, in the fifteenth century the invading Muslim armies desecrated and destroyed most of the temples and thereafter Bhubaneshwar fell into obscurity.

Although the temple town of Bhubaneshwar houses as many as five hundred temples, the Parsumareshwar, Mukteshwar, Rajarani, Brahmeshwar, Lingaraja, Vaitaldeul and Bindusagar group of temples deserve special mention.

The most obvious features of Orissan temples are the tall curvilinear towers or spires and a lower open structure or porch in front of the entrance of the tower. The taller tower is known as the *Deul* and the porch is referred to as *Jagmohan*. The interior of the sanctuary houses the deity and has a womb-like darkness to allow only a glimpse of the presiding deity. In later temples, two more halls were added. These comprised of *Natamandir* or dancing hall and the *Bhogmandir*, the hall of offerings.

Dedicated to Shiva, the Parsumareshwar temple built in the seventh century is the best preserved and most beautiful of Bhubaneshwar's early temples. The temple marks an important stage in the development of Hindu power and marks the transition from Buddhism to Hinduism in seventh century Orissa. The Shaivite sect was largely responsible for the conversion of Orissa to Hinduism in the fifth century. The tenth century Mukteshwar temple is often called the gem of Orissan architecture. Although incomplete, the twelve-century Rajarani temple is the finest among Bhubaneshwar's later temples. Rajarani does not have an image of the presiding deity and is no longer in use. The most unusual feature of this temple is the eighteen-meter high tower, which is surrounded by four miniature copies.

The largest group of temples is clustered around the Bindusagar tank. This small artificial lake mentioned in the Puranas is a place of great religious importance. The tank is believed to contain nectar, wine and water from the world's most sacred rivers. The Lingaraja deity is taken to the pavilion once every year for its ritual purificatory dip in one of the biggest ceremonies preformed there.

South of the Bindusagar stands the most stylisti-

cally evolved temple in all of Orissa, the Lingaraja temple. Built hundred years before the Jagannath temple, Lingaraja is one of India's most remarkable architectural achievements. The forty-five meter high *Deul* or tower of the temple is the main attraction that dominates the landscape. It features a rampant lion on its carved sides and the elephants beneath him signifying the triumph of Hinduism over Buddhism. The shrine has a thick *lingam* and is one of the twelve *jyotirlingas* in India. The temple has all the four main buildings in a typical Orissan temple style the *Deul*, *Jagmohan*, *Natamandir* and the *Bhogmandir*.

A number of places around Bhubaneshwar are worth a visit. The second century BC caves of Khandagiri and Udaigiri Jain caves offer a glimpse of the region's past before the rise of Hinduism. The rock edict of Emperor Ashoka at Dhauli commemorates the battle of 260 B.C., which consolidated his hold in the East and finally Pipli is famous for its appliqué work and colourful lampshades.

PURI

Puri, Orissa's prime temple town and tourist resort is the site of the famous Jagannath temple as well as the location of one of India's most spectacular religious festivals, the annual *Rath-yatra*. The temple of Jagannath, the Lord of the Universe, is the major attraction of Puri. To remain here for three days and three nights is considered particularly auspicious and the fact that Lord Jagannath does not discriminate between castes has made it extremely popular with the devotees.

The town rose to prominence as a religious centre when Shankaracharya, the religious teacher and philosopher, made it one of his four *Mathas* or centres for the practice of Hinduism. The Jagannath temple is one of the four most auspicious pilgrimage centres or *dhams*, abode of the divine, in India and thousands of devotees pour in every day to seek the blessings of the Lord who is an incarnation of Vishnu.

The temple is constructed in a typical Kalinga style consisting of the *Deul* or sanctuary with the *Jagmohan* or the audience hall in front of it, followed by the *Natamandir* or the dance hall, and the *Bhogmandir*, the hall of offerings. The wooden figures of the three deities Jagannath, Balabhadra and Subhadra stand in the sanctuary. The figure of the Lord is the unfinished work of the craftsman God, Vishwakarma, who in anger left this portrait of Lord Vishnu incomplete.

Built in twelfth century the Jagannath temple is the tallest in Orissa reaching a height of sixty-five meters and is crowned by the wheel of Vishnu and a flag. The temple is spread out in a spacious area and is enclosed within high outer walls. The outer wall has a gateway with pyramidal roofs on each side with two lions guarding the main entrance. On the East Side is the intricately carved, ten-meter high free-standing stone pillar with a small

One of the twelve wheels of the Konarak sun temple in the state of Orrisa

Seventy three percent of the Indian population lives in the villages. Each region has its own distinctive art form to decorate the dwellings made out of mud and cow dung.
Here in an Orrisan village one can see designs made out of rice paste decorating the doors and windows

figure of Arun, the charioteer of the Sun God. The Raja of Khurda moved this from its original site in Konarak. To the left of the main entrance is the temple kitchen that prepares fifty-six varieties of foods daily, making up the Bhog (offerings to the gods), and it is offered to the deity five times a day. The Mahaprasada is then distributed to thousands of devotees. During the Rath-yatra, which commemorates Krishna's journey from Gokul to Mathura, as many as 250,000 visitors are served daily.

The other major attraction of Puri is a long stretch of sun-kissed beach, which is relatively unspoiled, compared to most of the beaches in India that have fallen prey to commercialism.

KONARAK

The Sun Temple of Konarak, 35km north of Puri, marks the highest point of architectural achievement of the Kalinga style. Despite its present ruined state, it stands in majestic dignity in the midst of a vast stretch of sand a little away from the shore. The Sun temple was buried under a huge mound of sand and it was not until early this century, when the dune and heaps of collapsed masonry were cleared away that it was discovered. Like Bhubaneshwar, the name is evidently derived from the name of the presiding deity Konaraka, which means the *Arka*, sun, and *Kona*, which refers to the corner in which the temple was erected.

The main temple with its soaring 70m tower was called the Black Pagoda by the early European mariners, was an important landmark in their coastal voyage.

The temple had been conceived in the form of a colossal chariot for the Sun god *Surya*, its presiding deity. A team of seven galloping horses and twenty-four exquisitely carved wheels line the flanks of a raised platform of the main temple complex.

The temple complex consists of a sanctuary, its attached porch and an isolated pillared mandapa (hall). The whole temple was designed as the celestial chariot of the Sun God who according to Hindu mythology, courses across the sky in a chariot drawn by seven horses. As a giant model of *Surya's* war chariot, the temple was intended both as an offering to the Vedic Sun god and as a symbol for the passage of time itself, which lies in his control. The seven horses straining to haul the Sun eastwards in the direction of the dawn represent the days of the week, while the wheels along the base stand for the twelve months. The wheels have extraordinarily detailed friezes that run above and below them. These mainly depict military processions, hunting scenes and thousands of rampaging elephants.

An age-old legend narrates how Samba, son of lord Krishna, was very proud of his handsome looks, insulted a sage called Narada. One day, to take revenge Narada lured the prince to bathing ghat full of women. On reaching there, Samba indulged himself as much as he could.

The news of this wild orgy eventually reached Krishna's ears who cursed him into being a leper. The young prince was shattered. Finally twelve years of penance to Sun god brought relief. Later Samba erected the temple at Chandrabhaga to honour the sun god, Surya who cured him. This age-old tradition is still celebrated as the festival of *Magha Saptami,* in the month of January. Thousands of devotees gather here to bathe in the pond on the seventh day of the bright half of the month of *Magha* and absorb the curative powers of the sun at sunrise. Later they continue their worship of the nine planets at the temple. However, history attributes the founding of the temple to the eighteenth century Ganga monarch Narsimhadeva, who built the temple to commemorate his military success.

The main entrance to the temple complex is on the eastern side and directly in front lies the *Bhogamandapa* or the Hall of offerings. The ornate carvings of amorous couples, musicians and dancers on its pillars and platform suggest that it probably must have been used for ritual dance performances. Originally, a stone pillar crowned with an image of Aruna, Surya's charioteer also stood in front of the main door, though it has for some time now been moved to the eastern gateway to the Jagannath temple in Puri.

The porch or Jagmohana is the temple's main centrepiece. Its impressive pyramidal roof thirty-eight meter high is divided into three tiers with delicate carvings of musicians and dancers. There is also a figure of a four-headed, six-armed Shiva, garlanded with severed heads and performing the tandava or the dance of death. The exterior of the porch is decorated with elaborate sculptures in a profusion of animals, mythical beasts, deities and floral patterns. However, the main attraction continues to be the beautiful erotic sculptures. The erotic art was meant to be a metaphor for the ecstasy experienced by the soul when it unites with the divine cosmos.

Although the Jagmohana is the dominant building of the complex, the large scale of the sanctuary is still evident. The shrine contains a remarkable grey-green chlorite statue of *Surya*, which stands in sharp contrast with the surrounding yellowish orange Khondalite stone. However, the statue of the deity has long been removed to Jagannath Puri from the sanctum sanctorum. The central panel of the platform on which the deity stood contains a kneeling figure of King Narsimhadeva, the donor of the temple.

One of the most remarkable features of this temple is that the skill and craftsmanship is displayed down to the tiny details of stone carving. Each part of the temple, even to the smallest molding, has a prescribed name in the Orissan *Shilpa Shastra*.

Konarak hosts one of India's premier dance festivals each year in December, which draws both classical and folk dance groups from all over the country.

India is a photographer's delight. Walking around the streets one is rewarded with numerous photo opportunities
such as these in the streets of Calcutta
(Opposite page) To celebrate the annual festival of Durga Puja each locality in Calcutta buys the statues of goddess and worships them for
nine days amid huge fanfare. Later these works of art are immersed in the river Ganges

Visitors admire the tenth century Konarak temple that is shaped as the giant chariot of the sun god Surya
(Opposite page) Konarak temple surface is richly carved with erotic sculptures which symbolize the union of dynamic and static energies

south india

Nandi the bull is vehicle of lord Shiva, adorns the walls of the Shore Temple at Mahabalipuram
(Previous page) South India is known for its temple towns, sandy beaches, luxurious backwater cruises and the exciting snake
boat races, conducted during the Onam festival. About hundred oarsmen take positions in narrow snake like boat who's outer
surface is coated with thousands of eggs to help it glide faster
(Following page) Brass detail of a seventeenth century door

South India, bounded by the Indian Ocean in the south, the Bay of Bengal in the east and the Arabian Sea in the west, is largely comprised of the four Dravidian states of Kerala, Karnataka, Andhra Pradesh and Tamil Nadu (in India, language has been the criterion for the division of states). Though they are treated as a unit for convenience, and share certain basic similarities in outlook to the undiscerning visitor, they have distinct cultural and linguistic traditions. What we know as south

to be thriving centres of commerce for seafaring Arab traders in the fifteenth and sixteenth centuries. Kerala also had a strong Christian influence and was a base for missionary work. Hence, some of the largest concentrations of Christians in India are to be found here.

South India is known for its temples around which entire townships have sprung up. Unlike in the north, the temple in the south has not confined itself to being merely a place of worship but is responsible for setting moral standards and establishing village

MADRAS, KANCHIPURAM & MAHABALIPURAM

India does not necessarily conform to the location of the Tropic of Cancer, which runs through India and splits the country into two equal halves.

However, the Hindus here share a common preference for Murugan, Durga, Ganesha Shiva and Vishnu among the innumerable gods in the Hindu pantheon. Islam is predominant mostly in Hyderabad in Andhra Pradesh, where the Mughals had tried briefly to make inroads into the Deccan, and in some parts of coastal Kerala, the southernmost state, which used

assemblies, tribunals, banks, granaries, hospitals and schools around it, thereby serving as the custodian of society. This reflects in the conservative mores of the people, and probably explains why the temples are often in the very heart of the city.

The Dravidian influence in temple architecture and art has been strong in the south due to the relatively small role played by the Aryans. Each temple complex is a walled enclosure (*parikarma*) of concentric walls and corridors that houses markets, workshops, educational centres and living quarters. Every temple has towers (*gopurams*) that face the four cardinal points of the compass and serve as landmarks for travellers. Features that are associated with the temple itself include the water tank and flower garden, and a temple chariot that is drawn through the streets on festival days by hundreds of devotees with the deity mounted on it.

MADRAS

Madras now called Chennai, is the capital of the south Indian state of Tamil Nadu. Like the rest of the metro cities of India, its name also been changed under the new wave of local nationalism or politics. It is the home of the Tamil speaking population. It is the cradle of the Tamil literature, classical Indian dance, the Bharatnatyam and the Dravadian temple architecture. Madras is an odd mixture of cultures where the influences of British East India Company coexist with traditional Tamil culture. Therefore, it is not uncommon to find huge old colonial bungalows and churchyards jostling with temples and gigantic cinema and political hoardings for space and attention.

Culturally the south remained unaffected from the numerous invasions, which took place in the north of India. The south has thus preserved the Hindu way of life in its purest form. The major change came when the European traders started to outdo each other in the spice trade. Initially it was a race between the Portuguese and the Dutch. The French and the British imported the spices from these traders. When the prices were raised by them, it forced the British and later the French to start their own companies. Initially the Europeans were fighting with each other for their trading rights. As the competition grew fierce they started to dabble in local politics to assure their future. The Coromandel Coast saw numerous battles between the English and the French. Finally it was the British who emerged supreme. The Dutch were given the trading post of Tranquebar while the French held on to Pondicherry.

Fort St. George was the governing seat of the English. It was here that an unassuming clerk, Robert Clive, sowed the seeds of British Empire. With his financial and military genius he was soon able to control Bengal. Eugene Yale, founder of Yale University made his initial fortune as the Governor of Madras, in Fort St. George. His wedding took place at St. Mary's church in the Fort's compound. Very close to the Fort St. George is the Icehouse. It is in this building where ice was stored, imported by ship all the way from the East Coast of America.

Today this fourth largest city of India is outgrowing itself at a rapid pace. It is a busy metropolis with a thriving industry. Textiles, leather, InfoTech and

movies to name a few. Lately there has been a boom in automobile industry, with Koreans and Japanese finding the highly educated workforce in the port city as an attractive investment environment.

The tourist attractions of the city are few. The Hindu temple of Kapaleshvara in Myalapore dates back to the thirteenth century. It is dedicated to Lord Shiva. Legend has it that when Shiva was talking to his wife Parvati, he found her engrossed watching a peacock. This angered him and he transformed her into a peacock. Parvati in the form of peacock did number of penances to please her lord. Finally Shiva relented and changed her back to her beautiful self. The place is called *Mylapore* (Peacock place) to mark their reconciliation. It has a vast tank on the west where the devotees bathe on religious festivals. On the eastern entrance is a towering thirty-seven meter high technicolor *gopuram* (gateway). It is crowded with gods, goddesses and saints from the *Puranic* legends. There is a shrine depicting Parvati in the form of a peacock, worshipping *Shivalingam*. On the whole it is an excellent introduction to the temple life, sculpture and architecture of the south. This is amplified in great proportions in the other temple towns of Southern India.

Not far away from the temple of Mylapore is St. Thome cathedral. It is here the mortal remains of the doubting Thomas, apostle of Jesus Christ are said to be buried. The Hindu influence is evident with Christ standing on the lotus flower with peacocks on the either side. And the statue of Mary is draped in a *sari*.

The government museum is housed in a colonial building and has a fabulous collection of Chola bronzes. The most interesting place to visit in this city is Kalakshetra, the temple of art. Rukmani Devi Arundale, renowned *Bharatnatyam* danseuse of her time, founded it in 1936. She revived the classical dance form of Bharatnatyam and gave it respectability. A university set in a natural environment, it is dedicated to teach traditional art forms in traditional style. The morning prayer meeting of the students under the banyan tree is an enriching experience. The sights, which overshadow the monuments in Madras, are the temple town of Kanchipuram and shore temples of Mahabalipuram.

KANCHIPURAM

Kanchipuram is one of the seven holy cities of the Hindu pilgrim circuit; many also call it the Varanasi of South India, to drive home its importance. The city was founded by the great Pallava dynasty, which dominated the political scene of south India in the seventh and eighth century. The temple architecture spanning nearly a thousand years can be seen here. This "city of a Thousand Temples" boasts of temples dedicated to both Shiva and Vishnu. The Kailashnatha Temple, dedicated to lord Shiva, dates from 725 and was built during the reign of Rajasimha of the Pallava dynasty. This sandstone temple is remarkably well preserved. The main temple is enclosed by a wall, which houses numerous shrines. It is surrounded by a landscaped garden, with Nandi, vehicle of lord Shiva, occupying centre stage. The area around this temple is a landscape of a tranquil village life, with scenes of water buffalo and ducks lazying in the village pond. The only noise that disturbs this tranquility is from the rice mills and that of the looms of the silk weavers.

The temple, which dominates the skyline of Kanchipuram is the Ekambareshwra Temple. Its lofty gopurams of which tallest, is two hundred feet high. Kirshnadevaraya of Vijayanagar Empire built it in the sixteenth century. This Shiva temple has a long mandapa or the entrance hall. Inside the temple one can see the animal shaped chariots on which the idols of the deity are paraded through the streets of the temple town in the months of March and April. Other noteworthy temples are Vardhmana Temple and Kamakshi Temple. The former dates from the Chola period in the twelfth century and is dedicated to lord Vishnu. There is a beautiful *mandapa* (dance hall) on the edge of the tank. The columns are beautifully carved especially the ones with the riders on horseback and of Rati on a parrot. Kamakashi temple is dedicated to Parvati, consort of lord Shiva.

Kanchipuram, apart from being the temple town is also famous for its pure silk *sarees*. It is interesting to visit a weaver's hut and see some wonderful hues of silk yarn being transformed into intricate designs.

MAHABALIPURAM

Mahabalipuram, or Mamallapuram as it is known now was the port city of the Pallavas of Kanchipuram. The town is named after the Pallava ruler Narasimhavarman I who had excelled in wrestling, was awarded the title of the great wrestler.

The coastal village is more like an open-air museum. The monuments depict the evolution of the

Dravdian Style. Temple architecture elsewhere in the south has been greatly inspired by its finely sculptured, rock-cut monoliths (seventy in number) of which the most notable are the five rathas, named after classical Indian epic heroes of Mahabharta. These date back to the seventh century and were built during the reign of Narasimhavarman I. They could have been the prototypes of the later style of temple building. Carved out of the natural rock these incomplete works of art are arranged in a row like the temple chariots in the procession. There are some very fine sculptures on the walls and columns of these temples.

The Shore temple is the spectacular two-spired Pallava temple. Its similarity can be seen in Kailashnatha temple of Kanchipuram. The Shore temple is attributed to Rajasimha who built it in the eighth century. It has shrines dedicated to both Vishnu and Shiva. The sea breeze down the centuries has taken its toll on the sculptures of the temple. One can still make out the scores of Nandi bulls, which decorate the surrounding walls.

The most spectacular monument of Mahabalipurm is the Descent of the Ganges or Arjuna's Penance. It is world's largest bas-relief (80ft x 27ft) engraved on steep hillside. The sculptures on the rock face are the mixture of gods, yogis and animals and are depicted with great sensitivity. Originally there used to be a natural waterfall depicting Ganges in the narrow cleft of the relief, but it has since dried up. The yogi standing on one foot with his arms raised towards the heaven is believed to be Arjuna doing penance to obtain a boon from Shiva. In other interpretation he is identified as sage Bhagirath who requests Shiva to let the Ganges descend into his matted hair and from there onto earth and wash away the ashes of his ancestors, thus giving them liberation.

Mahabalipuram is a charming, laid-back place. All the major attractions are within walking distance, separated by the sculptors' workshops. The sounds of their chisel and hammer give the impression that the creative energy never left this coastal village.

Five Ratahas, is a group of five incomplete temples at Mahabalipuram, near Madras, that show the evolution of South Indian temple architecture.

*A pond in Kanchipuram reflects the tranquil village life, fisherman, ducks,
water buffaloes getting a bath and the Gopuram or the temple gateway in the background*

A sculptor carves out a statue of Hindu divinity from a piece of rock thereby carrying out the centuries old tradition of Mahabalipuram
(Opposite page) Mahabalipuram boasts of worlds largest and most magnificent bas-relief, dating back to seventh century,
known as Arjuna's Penance or the descent of the Ganges.
The sculptures on the rock face are the mixture of gods, yogis and animals and are depicted with great sensitivity.

View of the golden vimana and multicoloured gopurams at Ranganatha Temple in Trichy
(Following page) detail of the pillar at the entrance of a temple

Tiruchirapalli also known as Trichy is situated in the heartland of Tamil Nadu and lies in the Kaveri delta. The town is best known for the spectacular Ranganathaswamy Temple in Srirangam, a small village nestled on the island of the river Cavery. A Chola fortification from the second century, it came to prominence under the Nayaks who built the dramatic Rock Fort and firmly established Trichy as a trading city. However, owing to its strategic position, Trichy was always caught between warring factions. The Vijaynagar kings who in turn were overcome by the Muslims crowning the hilltop.

The Ranganathaswamy Temple at Srirangam, six kilometers north of Trichy is among the most revered shrines of Vishnu in south India. The temple is famous for its superb structure, the twentyone majestic *gopurams* and its rich collection of temple jewellery. The *gopurams* increase in size from the centre onwards. The exquisite central tower is the main attraction, which crowns the main sanctuary and is coated in gold and carved with images of Vishnu's incarnations on each of its four sides.

TRICHY, TANJORE, GANGAIKONDACHOLAPURAM, DARASURAM

ousted the Cholas. Then came the Nayaks and after nearly a century of struggle against the French and the British, the town came under the British control.

The looming structure of the Rock Fort dominates the landscape of Trichy. The fort is built on a massive eighty-four meter high, sand-coloured rock. The Pallavas were the first to start construction with later additions made by the Nayaks. The entrance is from the China bazaar, a long flight of red and white painted steps cut steeply uphill, past a series of Pallava and Pandya rock cut temples, to the Vinayak temple

The temple town of Srirangam stands on an island in the Kaveri River and is surrounded by seven concentric walled courtyards, with magnificent gateways and several shrines. The outer three walls form the hub of the temple community, where ascetics, priests and musicians stay. The fourth wall contains some of the finest and oldest buildings of the complex including a temple to the goddess Ranganayaki where the devotees worship before approaching Vishnu's shrine. On the East Side is the heavily carved Thousand-Pillared Hall or *Kalyana Mandapa*, constructed in the Chola period.

Sheshagiriraya Mandapa, south of the Kalyana Mandapa, features pillars profusely decorated with rearing steeds and hunters, representing the triumph of good over evil.

The dimly-lit inner shrine, the most sacred part of the temple, shelters the image of Vishnu in his aspect of Ranganath, reclining on the serpent Adisesha. The entrance to the shrine is from the south, but for one day each year, during the festival of Vaikunth Ekadasi, the northern gate is opened and is considered propitious for those who pass through it.

Most of the present structure dates from the fourteenth century, when the temple was renovated and enlarged after the Muslims attack. Spread over more than sixty hectares, the temple complex lacks any planning since different rulers between the fourteenth and the seventeenth centuries expanded it.

TANJORE, GANGAIKONDACHOLAPURAM AND DARASURAM

These are the three gems of the Chola architecture. Their sheer size and beauty reflects the power of the Cholas who held sway over the south for many centuries.

Tanjore or Thanjavur contains many exquisite temples of which the tallest ancient monument in India is the Brihadeshwara Temple. This temple marks the zenith of the Chola architecture. The city attained prominence under the Cholas in the ninth century. The Brihadeshwara Temple dedicated to Shiva, is a symbol of the greatness of the Chola Empire under King Rajaraja I. The temple is the most ambitious of the architectural enterprises of the Cholas and a fitting symbol of the magnificent achievements of Rajaraja I whose military campaigns spread Hinduism to the Maldives, Java and Srilanka.

The Chola kings were great patrons of art, literature, sculpture music and dance and majority of the temples in Tanjore have been built during their reign. Although all the ninety-three temples of Tanjore are beautiful in their own right, none command the majestic presence of the Brihadeshwara Temple.

The Brihadeshwara Temple is one of the most magnificent World Heritage monuments in the country. Its thirteen story, sixty-six meter high *vimana* is the tallest in India and is topped by a dome carved from a block of granite, which is so cleverly designed that it never casts a shadow at noon throughout the year. The dome weighs eighty tons and is believed to have been hauled up a six-kilometer long ramp.

The courtyard features an enormous *Nandi* guarding the entrance of the sanctuary. It is carved out of a single block of granite and is six-meter long. The main temple is constructed of granite and consists of a long-pillared hall, *mandapa*, followed by the *ardhamandapa* or half- hall, which leads to the inner sanctum or the *garbha griha*. The architecture, sculpture and paintings are all exceptional. Profuse inscriptions and beautiful sculptures of Shiva, Vishnu and Durga grace the three sides of the massive base of the

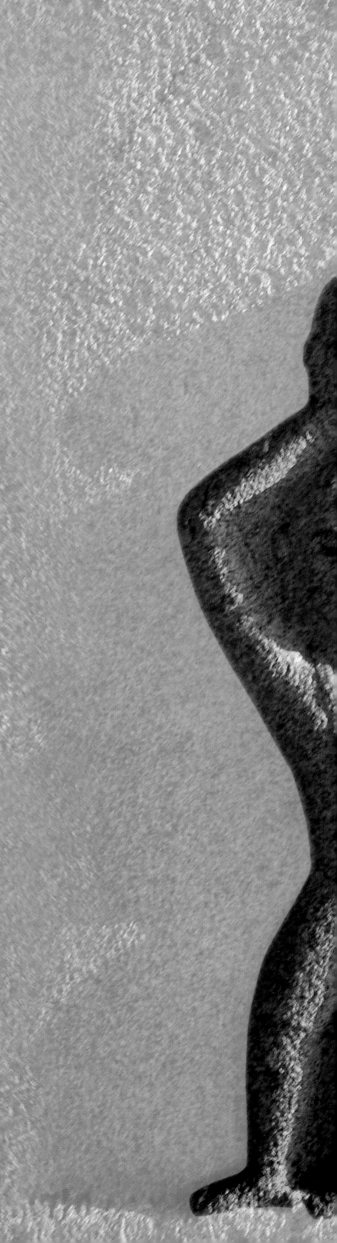

shrine. There are detailed carvings of dancers showing eighty one different *Bharatnatyam* poses and are the first to record classical dance form in this manner.

The passage surrounding the garbha griha contains some of south India's greatest art treasures, a frieze of beautiful frescoes of deities, celestials and dancing girls from the reign of Rajaraja I. These were hidden for nearly one thousand years under the Nayaka paintings from the seventeenth century.

A little away from the Brihadeshwara Temple is the Royal Palace Compound, where members of the erstwhile royal family still reside. The Nayaks started construction of the palace in the sixteenth century and later it was completed by the Marathas. The Royal Museum near the entrance of the complex houses a small collection of manuscripts costumes, musical instruments and weapons used by the royal family. Its Durbar Hall is of particular interest, which has some Chola bronzes on display.

The Saraswati Mahal Library in the palace is one of the most important oriental manuscript collections in India. It contains over forty thousand rare books, several of which are first editions. The majority of the manuscripts are in Sanskrit, including many on palm-leafs. The Tamil works include treatises on medicine and works from Sangam period.

Tanjore is also famous for its bronze statues, Carnatic classical music and Bharatnatyam dance. Chola bronzes, a unique art form of Tamil Nadu have become popular enough to penetrate the world market. The icon of Nataraja, or the dancing Shiva, is one of the most recognizable Indian symbols.

Rajendra I of Chola dynasty built Bhideshvara temple in the village of Gangaikondacholapuram in the eleventh century. It commemorates his successful campaign up to river Ganga in eastern India. The village too takes its name from this victory. On the outset it looks like a replica of the Bhideshwara Temple of Tanjore but is much smaller in scale and size. There is a giant linga in the sanctum below the giant *vimana*. The temple walls have beautiful sculptures of Hindu divinity. The most beautiful one is in the north entrance, where Shiva seated along his consort Parvati is bestowing a wreath on Chandesha. There are smaller shrines in the compound and a giant Nandi at the entrance. The temple is set in a beautiful landscaped garden maintained by the archaeological department.

Airavateshvara Temple at Darasuram is attributed to Rajaraja II who built it in twelfth century. Although smaller in size than the other two Chola temples, Darasuram is described as a sculptor's dream in stone. The proportions and grace in the figures is unsurpassed in the south. The front mandapa itself is in the form of a huge chariot drawn by horses and elephants. The columns are carved out of a single block of granite and depict mythological stories. In front of the temple are stone panels, which produce musical notes when struck. The paintings on the roof in the small museum of the temple are simply exquisite.

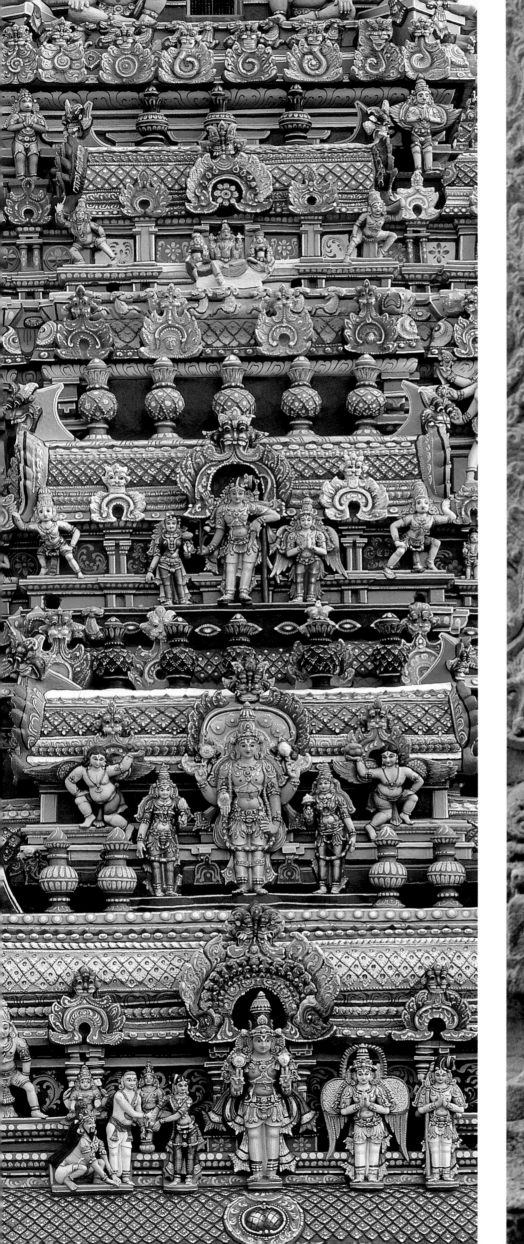

(Previous page left) Multicoloured gopuram hallmark of south Indian Dravidian style, Trichy
(Previous page right) Beautifully carved columns adorn the mandapa of Ranganatha temple in Trichy

*Brihadeshwara temple of Tanjore dates back to ninth century and marks the zenith of Chola architecture,
its sixty-six meter vimana is tallest in south India
(Opposite page) Shiva seated with his consort Parvati laying the wreath on his disciple, eleventh century, Gangaikondacholapuram*

Thousands of Shivalingas in Shiva's shrine at Brihadeshwara Temple, Tanjore
(Opposite page) A temple chariot shaped as a lion, these are used to cart the statues of the deity in the city during the temple festival

Although smaller in proportion, Airavatesvara temple at Darasuram is the well preserved gem of the Chola architecture,
it was built in twelveth century and is attributed to Rajaraja II

Chinese fishing nets as seen at the sunset from the promenade in Cochin
(Following page) Details of the painting on the roof of the Meenakshi temple, Madurai

Madurai, the ancient home of Tamil culture is the seat of the famous temple dedicated to Meenakshi and Sundereshwar. One of the oldest cities in south Asia, Madurai is situated on the banks of the River Vaigai. It has been an important centre of worship and commerce from as far back as the sixth century. Ancient Madurai was also a centre of Tamil culture, famous for its writers, poets and temple builders and was the literary and cultural centre during the last three Sangam periods or literary academics.

the patronage of the Nayaks and the city was rebuilt on the pattern of a lotus centreing on the Meenakshi Temple. The Nayaks ruled the city until the eighteenth century when eventually the British took over.

The Meenakshi Temple is an outstanding example of Vijaynagar temple architecture. The nine massive *gopurams* of this vast complex are profusely decorated and some believe that there are as many as 33 million carvings that include a plethora of dancing poses. The temple is dedicated to Meenakshi, Shiva's consort. The

MADURAI, COCHIN, KOVALAM

Madurai was the capital of the Pandyan Empire for about a thousand years. It became a major commercial city and trade with Greece, Rome and China flourished. The Pandya capital fell in the tenth century, when the Cholas gained control over the area. There was a short period in which the Muslim Sultans ruled Madurai. Malik Kafur completely destroyed the city in 1310 plundering and desecrating most of the temples. Subsequently the Vijaynagar kings captured it in 1364 until the Nayaks asserted their independence. Madurai flourished under

temple is named after the daughter of a Pandyan king who, according to legend, was born with three breasts. At the time of the birth, the king was told that the extra breast would disappear, when she met the man she was supposed to marry, and this happened when she met Lord Shiva on Mount Kailash. Shiva arrived in Madurai, later, in the form of Lord Sundereswara, and married her.

As Meenakshi is the presiding deity of the temple the daily ceremonies are first performed in her shrine and unlike other temples Sundereshwar or Shiva plays a secondary role. Every night the idol of Sundereshwar is taken to the temple of Meenakshi, the fish-eyed goddess, so that they can spend the night together.

The temple has a relatively small entrance and to the left are steps leading down to the sacred tank of the Golden Lotus. To the west of the tank is the pavilion leading to the Meenakshi shrine. The roof of the passage in front of the shrine is painted with numerous Ganesha figures. The passages are full of pilgrims, performing puja or finalizing marriages. The pillars of this pavilion are carved in the form of mythical beasts or *yali*, a common feature in temples throughout this region. The Meenakshi shrine stands in its own enclosure surrounded with smaller shrines. The Sundereshwar shrine lies north of the tank within another enclosure and with smaller *gopurams* on four sides.

The Thousand- pillared Hall is another main feature of the temple in the northeast corner of the complex. Each column is richly carved and detailed images of Parvati as a huntress playing the veena and Shiva riding a peacock are particularly fascinating. It also houses the art museum, which exhibits brass and stone images and friezes. Although these exhibits are interesting the five musical pillars carved out of a single stone definitely steal the show. Each pillar produces a different note on being tapped.

The temples in ancient times were not just limited to worship. Apart from religion, it provided scope for a justice court, a treasure house, and an institution to impart ethical education and fostered various arts including music and dance. The temple is a hive of activity at any given day in the year. More than 15,000 people visit it everyday with the numbers swelling to 25,000 on Friday, sacred to the goddess Meenakshi.

The Thirumalai Nayaka Palace, a kilometer away from the Meenakshi Temple was built by the most illustrious of the Nayak Kings and parts of it still survive. Much of the palace was dismantled by Thirumalai's grandson and used for a new palace at Tiruchirapalli. The original complex had a shrine, an armory, a theater, royal quarters, a harem, armory and gardens. Mariamman Teppakkulam Tank, few kilometers east of the old city, is the site for Teppam Festival (Float Festival) in the months of January and February.

COCHIN

Kerala, the land of coconut and spice, is also the greenest state in the country with its backwaters and palm trees. The people of Kerala are a harmonious mixture of Hindu, Muslim and Christian communities. It is reputed for its sandy beaches, luxurious backwater cruises and the exciting snake boat races, conducted during the Onam festival. Chinese fishing nets, elegant Kathakali dancers and curative aryuvedic massages are other compelling features of this state.

Cochin is the most enchanting city of Kerala. Its natural harbour has attracted voyagers since the Roman times. Its proximity to the tea, rubber, coffee and spices plantations has made it the commercial capital of Kerala. It used to be an important centre of the sea route between Europe and China. The Chinese influence is said to date back to the times of Kublai Khan when they introduced the unique Chinese fishing nets. The presence of the Chinese must have been quite prominent which is reflected in the vast quantities of Chinese pickle jars and antiques that are available. The culture of the city is very cosmopolitan, with influences of the Chinese, Jews, Arabs, Portuguese, Dutch and the English contributing to it. This flavor is still evident in the Fort Cochin area, which houses an incredible number of colonial buildings. Fortunately it has been spared from the building frenzy, which can be seen in the Ernakulam region of the city.

The eventful history of this city began when a major cyclonic flood of 1341 opened the estuary at Cochin, till then a land-locked region, turning it into one of the finest natural harbours in the world. As a result, voyagers looked forward to visit this first truly international port of the Indian peninsula. Vasco da Gamma, who discovered the sea route to India, lived in Fort Cochin. The Dutch ousted Portuguese in 1633 and finally the British took control of Princess of the Arabian Sea, as the sailors lovingly called the city, from the Dutch in 1795.

Chinese fishing nets along the promenade in the fort Cochin are the most photogenic landmarks of Cochin. The nets are erected on teak wood and bamboo poles and their working is controlled by huge stones tied to the other end to provide a counter balance. These nets were brought here in the fourteenth century by the Chinese traders from the Court of Kubla Khan. During the high tide the area is buzzing with activity. The seafood shops sell their fresh catch, which you can buy and get cooked in one of the numerous stalls close by.

The Santa Cruz Basilica, was built originally by the Portuguese and elevated to a Cathedral by Pope Paul IV in 1558. Luckily, it was spared by the Dutch conquerors who destroyed many other Catholic buildings. Later the British demolished the structure and Bishop Dom Gomez Vereira commissioned a new building in 1887. Consecrated in 1905, Santa Cruz was proclaimed a Basilica by the Pope John Paul II in 1984.

Many of the old colonial buildings in the Fort area have been lovingly restored retaining the colonial flavour, and opened as hotels. A few minutes ride from Fort Cochin is the Mattencherry or the Jew Town. It is famous for its Dutch Palace, built by the Portuguese for the Hindu king in order to gain trading rights. Later the Dutch restored it. It is an interesting museum with fabulous frescoes based on the Hindu epics painted on the walls. The highlight of this section is the Synagogue, the oldest in Asia. It has colorful ambiance with painted Chinese blue tiles on the floor and dozens of colorful chandeliers hanging from the ceiling. The Synagogue street houses the few remaining families of Cochin Jews. It was once a dynamic community who excelled as the middlemen between the Europeans and the local population. The area is fast becoming a haven for antique dealers. Nearby some old warehouses still deal with traditional spices. The strong aroma emanating from them will guide you to their door.

Portuguese Franciscan Friars built St. Francis Church in 1503. It is one of India's oldest churches. Initially it was built as a wooden structure, later the Portuguese replaced it with a permanent stone structure. During the Portuguese rule, it remained a Roman Catholic Church right up to seventeenth century. Later, the Dutch converted it into a reformist church (1664 – 1804) and finally the British made it into an Anglican church from 1804. Today it is known by the name of the Church of South India (CSI).

Another important fact about the church is that Vasco Da Gamma, who died in 1524, was buried here before his mortal remains were taken to Portugal fourteen years later. The church has an airy feeling about it with big windows and huge punkhas, old style fans operated by a person sitting outside the room with the help of a rope.

Today Cochin is a rich trade centre, a major military base, a busy port, a great shipbuilding centre and a centre for Christianity. It has also the swankiest airport of India. The wealth of the city and its surrounding area can be gauged by the numerous jewellery shops that can be seen everywhere. No trip to Cochin is complete unless you cruise down the backwaters of Allepey and drive up to Tekkady, probably the most scenic route of India. If you have time and the inclination then the beaches of Kovalam are a good place to unwind with Kerela's famed *Aryuvedic* massages.

Oldest synagogue in India is in Cochin. It is decorated with hand painted Chinese tiles and colourful chandeliers.
Jewish community dominated the spice trade on the Malabar Coast. Migration to Israel has reduced the community
to a few hundred

The golden flag staff in front of Sudeshwar shrine in Madurai's Meenakshi Temple
(Opposite page) Bronze door at the entrance to Meenakshi Temple in Madurai. Faithful light oil lamps before entering the Hindu temple
In south Indian temples the shrines of the deities are till today illuminated by oil lamps only

South Indian temples are vibrant with life, pilgrims in their colourful silk sarees add gaiety to the ambiance
(Opposite page) Marriages can be seen conducted in the corridors of Meenakshi Temple, Madurai

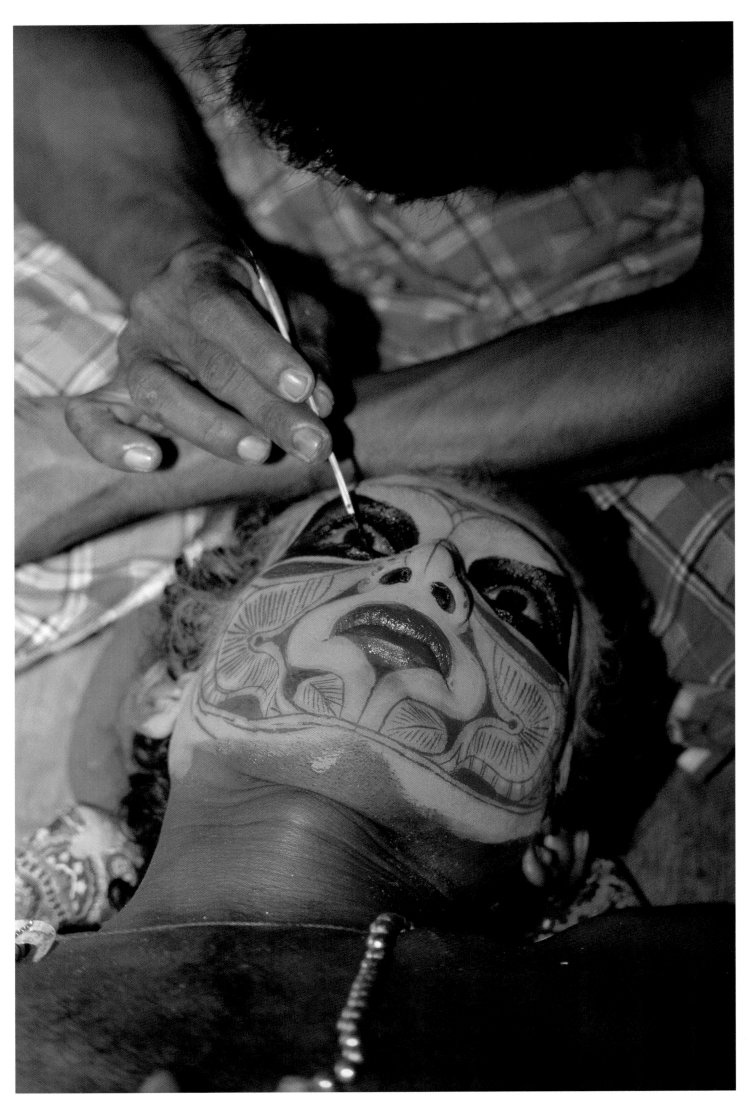

Two performers from Kerala getting ready for their respective performance. On the top is the artist getting traditional makeup of the religious dance drama called the Theyyam. On the right is the performer, in tiger hunter's garb, participating in the Phulikuli dance celebrated at the time of harvest festival, Onam

*(Following page) Fishermen are waiting for the catch at the Chinese fishing nets in Cochin.
These nets were brought by the Chinese traders during the times of Kubali Khan in the fifteenth century*

215

Pilgrims visiting the Channa-Keshva temple in Belur
(Previous page) Kovalam in southern Kerala is world renowned for its exotic beaches and rejuvenating Aryuvedic massages
(Page before previous page) A Cruise along the Kerala's backwaters is rewarded with the lush green scenery
and an insight to the life on the waterways
(Following page) The Hoysala temples are richly adorned
with fine carvings of the Hindu epics such as this frieze of Ramayana in Hoysaleshwara temple at Halebid

Mysore, with the Palace of the Maharaja, continues to be the centre of cultural life in Karnataka. Henry Irwin built the palace in an Indo-Saracenic style of grand proportions in 1912, for Maharaja Krishnaraja Wadiyar IV. It is one of the largest palaces in the country, beautifully restored and maintained. The Palace hosts the world famous *Dussehra* festival every year in the month of October. The former princely state of Mysore is also famous for its sandalwood and jasmine gardens.

The majestic Elephant gate is the main entrance to the

and Bohemian chandeliers.

An Italian marble staircase leads to the magnificent Darbar hall, a grand colonnaded hall with lavishly framed paintings by famous Indian artists including Raja Ravi Varma. The massive hall affords views across the parade ground and gardens to Chamundi hill. The Maharaja gave audience from here seated on a throne made from 280kgs of solid Karnatakan gold. The jewel encrusted golden throne with its ornate steps was originally made of fig wood decorated with ivory before it was embellished with gold, silver and jewels.

MYSORE, SOMNAHTPUR, BELUR, HALEBID

centre of the palace and bears the Mysore royal symbol of the double-headed eagle, now the state emblem. The elaborately decorated, gem-studded elephant *howda* made of 84-kg gold is of particular interest and is used to carry the deity during Dussehra.

The octagonal *Kalyan Mandap*, the royal wedding hall south of the courtyard has a beautiful stained glass ceiling and magnificently detailed oil paintings illustrating the great Mysore *Dussehra* festival of 1930. This opulent hall still houses some of the finest Belgian crystal, silver furniture

The passage through the beautifully inlaid wood and ivory door of the Ganesh temple leads to the Ambavilas, the private audience hall. This extraordinary decorated hall features beautiful stained glass and gold leaf paintings. Three richly decorated doors lead into the Diwan-i-khas. The central silver door depicts Vishnu's ten incarnations and the eight Dikpalas or the directional guardians.

The Jaganmohan Palace, a little further west of the Maharaja's palace was used as a royal residence until Krishnaraja Wadiyar IV turned it into a picture gallery and museum in 1915. The ground floor displays costumes, musical instruments and numerous portraits and photographs. A series of nineteenth and twentieth century paintings dominate the first floor. The work of Raja Ravi Varma is particularly interesting, because he was first to introduce modern techniques in Indian art.

Devraja market is a tourist's delight. It has numerous stalls selling fruits, vegetables, colourful *kumkum* used by Hindu women in the parting of their hair to announce their maritial status, and jasmine flowers being sold by the kilos. Incense and spice shops abound this colourful market place.

Chamundi hill, immediately to the southeast of the city, is topped with a temple of Durga, Chamundeshwari, the chosen deity of the Mysore Rajas. This twelfth century temple features a Chamundi figure of solid gold. Outside in the courtyard, stands a fearsome statue of the demon buffalo, Mahishasur. A little further downhill is a magnificent five-meter Nandi, Shiva's bull, which dates back to the seventeenth century.

Hoysalas, who were the feudal lords of the Chalukyas of Kalyani, became independent in the eleventh century and founded a new dynasty with their name. They constructed magnificent temples in Halebid, Belur and Somnathpur. Hoysala temples stand out more for their sculptural workmanship rather than architectural achievements.

The three temples Halebid, Belur and Somnathpur, situated in the state of Karnatka, are considered the gems of Hoysala architecture. The hallmark of these temples are the star-shaped platforms with wide circumambulatory space on which they are built.

The Hoysala temple consists of a *vimana*, connected by a short *antrala* to a closed *navaranga* which is proceeded by *mandapa*. The temple walls have many triangular folds, which gave artists more surface area to exhibit their skills on, and also the play of light and shadow is thus more amplified. The carvings are so fine and delicate that at the first glance they appear to have been done on sandalwood. Nowhere in India, the temples are so intricately carved as are these three. Every square inch of their walls is lavishly decorated with figures of gods and goddesses, along with an elaborate foliage design on each divinity. The remaining surface is covered with Hindu epics of Mahabharata and Ramayana. Armies of soldiers and animals cover the lower part of the temple. Another noteworthy feature is the lathe-turned columns, which adorn the temple hall and circumventor passages.

The temples were built between the twelfth and thirteenth century by the Hoysala dynasty. The origin of the name of the dynasty is a heroic legend, in which Sala, the founder of the dynasty, kills a tiger single-handedly. This story can be seen translated into a sculpture of Sala fighting the tiger at all temples. Unlike other temples of India that are made out of granite or sandstone, Hoysala temples are made with softer dark grey green chlorite schist, which is conducive to fine carving and hardens with the passage of time. No wonder that details of the sculptures are simply exquisite. So minute are the carvings that even the details such as jewellery worn by the divinities, the rings on the fingers, the nails, or as in one statue the bracelet of the dancer is free to rotate on her wrist. After the destruction of Halebid at the hands of the Muslims a new capital, Belur, was established close by.

Belur

Belur's religious importance can be understood as it is compared to the holy city of Varanasi by the local people who proudly refer to it as *Dakshin* (the southern) Varanasi.

It is said that King Vishnuvardhana after defeating the

mighty Cholas of South built the temple of Channa-Keshava. The temple is dedicated to Vijaya Narain, an incarnation of Vishnu, and was built in 1117. According to inscriptions, the temple was built to commemorate his conversion from Jainism to Vaishnavism.

The surface of the temple is filled with friezes of Vishnu, stories of Puranas and other Hindu epics, carved out in minutest details. Celestial beauties, *Mandakins*, are carved into brackets supporting the overhanging eaves.

These sculptures epitomizing feminine grace are the finest example of the Hoysala art. The lady dressing herself, the lady with the mirror, the lady with the parrot and the huntress are noteworthy for their feminine grace and beauty. Inside the temple one of the columns was adorned with a map of the temple and this giant column was freely rotating on its axis!! The carvings on it can still be seen, but erosion has now jammed its free movement. The temple is a veritable museum of sculpture and intricate floral carving.

Among the Hoysala temples, Channa-Keshava is the only living one. The other two, Halebid and Somnathpur, do not have ritual service. For this reason the temple is buzzing with life and religious ceremonies. In the large courtyard one can see subsidiary shrines and temple chariots in the shapes of various animals adding colour to the temple. The Vijyanagara kings contributed the entrance tower on the east side at a later date.

Halebid

Halebid, the ancient Hoysala capital, houses the ornate Hoysaleswara temple that dates back to the twelfth century. It was built by Ketamalla, a minister of Vishnuvardhana, the Hoysala ruler, and is dedicated to Lord Shiva. He also built the Belur temple and the Mahabaleshwar temple at Chamundi Hills near Mysore. The temple surpasses both of them in architecture and refinement of sculptures.

Halebid's decline set in when it was sacked by the Muslim general Malik Kafur in early fourteenth century. After the attack, the city never regained its former glory. Today, only a handful tourists come to see the beauty of this secluded Hoysala masterpiece. The twin temples are connected by a passage on the inside with a dance hall or *mandapa* on either end. There is a statue of a giant *Nandi*, vehicle of lord Shiva facing the temple. Elaborate carvings decorate entire face of the temple.

SOMNATHPUR

Somnathpur is smallest of the three Hoysala temples. It was built Somnatha, an official under the Hoysala King Narasimha III (1254-1291). It is an excellent introduction to Hoysala art and architecture. Although the carvings are not as elaborate as its predecessors at Halebid and Belur, it makes up for it by surviving in its original form. It stands on a raised star shaped platform in the centre of a rectangular courtyard having sixty-four cells and a passage supported with lathe-turned columns. The temple is unique with its three *shikhars* (*trikutachala*), three *garbahgirahs* and three *antralas* joined to a comman *navaranga*. The ceiling inside the temple is remarkable with the keystone of the sixteen domes sculpted as a banana flower in different stages of flowering. Outside, the walls of the temple have been profusely decorated with friezes of gods and goddesses, Puranic and epic scenes. The majority of the sculptures are attributed to the artist Mallithamma. The inscriptions in the temple give details of construction and mention the grants given for the upkeep of the temple. There is a back staircase to the roof from where one can view the surroundings. This bird's eye view never fails to impress the viewer, with its unique star-shaped composition of this temple.

(Previous page) In the nineteenth and twentieth century Indian maharajas tried to out do each other by building outlandish palaces often imitating the ones they saw in Europe such as Laitmahal in Mysore

(Above) Golden nagaraja provides shelter to the deity in Channa-KeshvaTemple, Belur
(Opposite page) Giant nandi facing the Hoysaleshwara temple in Halebid

The hallmark of the Hoysala temple architecture is the star shaped platforms on which they are built in the centre of the courtyard, such as Somnathpur temple near Mysore
(Opposite page) Hoysala temples are richly carved with intricate sculpture of gods, goddesses and the Hindu epics. Flora and fauna is depicted with great exuberance such as the Hoysaleshwara temple at Halebid

*Magic of dawn at Hampi: a panoramic view of the Hampi landscape with the towering gopuram of
Virupaksha temple as seen from Hemakuta Hill.
"A beautiful city as large as Rome and with all facilities to its five hundred thousand citizens"
... wrote Domingo Paes a Portuguees traveller on Hampi in the year 1521
(Following page) A shrine in the courtyard of the Vitthala Temple, Hampi*

If there were a competition among the most exotic sights of India, Hampi would be a serious contender for the first place. This city of victory, Vijyanagara, is set in a surreal landscape of large smooth boulders that have miraculously hung in balance through centuries. In this awesome theater of nature are ruins of the Vijyanagar, spread in the area of twenty-six square kilometers. The history of the site gains importance with the Vijayanagar dynasty in the fourteenth century. Two brothers, Harihara and Bukka, laid the foundation of the empire in 1336.

The monkey kings Vali and Sugriva of the Hindu epic Ramayana are believed to have ruled close to Hampi. Sugriva and Hanuman were driven out of the kingdom by Vali. Taking pity on the plight of the monkey chiefs, Rama eliminated Vali and restored the kingdom to Sugriva. A huge mound of scorious ash in the adjacent village is believed to be the cremation site of Vali. Rama lived in Hampi while the monkey chief Hanuman went to look for Sita in Lanka, the capital of the demon king Ravana.

The most imposing religious building of Hampi is

HAMPI, BADAMI, AIHOLE, PATTADAKAL

Later Bukka's son Harihara II not only consolidated the empire but also brought Sri Lanka and Burma under Vijayanagra's control. Later in the early sixteenth century, Vijayanagar entered its golden era under the rule of Kishnadevaraya. He had visitors from Persia, Italy and Portugal at his court. All of them speak of the splendors of his empire and the affluence of its citizens. He erected some of the most important temples of the city. The giant monolithic image of Laxmi Narashima (Vishnu's avatar) is attributed to him.

the Vitthala Temple. It is situated on the southern bank of the Tungabhadra River and was built during the reign of Devaraya II in the mid fifteenth century. It is located in a rectangular enclosure within which stands the main temple, *kalyan mandapa* and *utsav mandapa*. Mahamandapa is decorated with sculptured friezes of horses and warriors. Of the fifty-six columns, the ones outside are decorated with Narasimha figures while female dancers and musicians decorate the ones inside. The ceiling is carved with beautiful lotus motifs. The temple shows the zenith of

Vijayanagra art and architecture.

A marvel of Vijayanagra art is the stone chariot, which is located in front of the main shrine, which is dedicated to *Garuda*, the vehicle of Vishnu, the mythological half- bird-half-man. It is the precise replica of the wooden temple chariot, but here it has been translated into stone. The minutest details have been incorporated into the carving and designed so much so that once it was possible to rotate the stone wheels of this magnificent *Ratha*. Two elephants are carved in the front appear to be ready to pull the *Ratha* to any distance.

Southwest of the temple are the ruins of the King's balance. On auspicious days the king was weighed against gold and precious stones that was later distributed among the citizens. To see the sunrise over the Viruprakasha temple from the Hemkuta hill is an unforgettable experience. Hampi is one of those places in the world where you feel that any amount of time spent there is not enough.

BADAMI, AIHOLE & PATTADAKAL

Situated along the Malprabha River in the lower Deccan region these ancient sites of the Chalukyan capital date between the sixth and the eighth century. During the reigns of Pulukesin I and his son Pulukesin II, of the Chalukyan dynasty, there seems to have been a flow of creative energy, not witnessed ever before in the history. More than two hundred temples were built during this period. But only some fifty odd survive the ravages of time. They represent Hindu, Jain and Buddhist faiths. The temples showcase the transition of rock cut cave temples to that of free standing ones. It is the birthplace of temple architecture of India. Dravidian, Jain, Buddhist, Hoysala and Nagar styles can be seen in their emerging stages, which finally culminated in mighty Kailasha Temple of Ellora.

AIHOLE

Aihole, inscriptions refer to it as Aryapura, occupies a unique place in the history of the temple architecture of India. It was the experimental ground for the Early Chalukyan kings (450-750) to build structural temples from mid fifth century onwards.

Within the ancient fortification there are fifty temples and the same amount exists outside. Most of the temples were originally dedicated to Vishnu but later converted to a worship of the Shiva cult.

The earlier temples are of pavilion type with a slightly sloping roof. The first phase of early Chalukyan temple architecture ended with construction of Meguti Temple, which incidentally is the first structural temple (634) in India. An inscription on the temple mentions the great poet, Kalidas in the court of Chandra Gupta Maurya.

Further experimentations in giving a cognate shape to the temple roof by adding towers resulted in evolving three distinctive styles namely: *Daravida*, *Nagra* and *Kadamba-Nagra* of which latter is a more evolved form of *Dravida* style and is evident in Badami and Pattadakal temples.

The Durga temple is unique in conception on account of its apsidal plan but with non-apsidal curvilinear sikhara. Its name is misleading as it is dedicated to the sun god Surya and not to goddess Durga. It is named so as it was within the walls of a fort (*Durg*). The structural art of these temples is full of vigour. There are also some Jain temples belonging to the later Rashtrakuta period.

PATTADAKAL

Pattadakal was the second strong hold of the Early Chalukyas and served as the capital between seventh and eighth century. It is located on the banks of the river Malaprabha not very far from Aihole. The architecture shows the continuation of the evolution of both Dravadian style and the Nagar style temples from Aihole. The temples here are dedicated to Shiva, Hindu lord of destruction. The sculptures on the temples ornately depict the societal life of the early Chalukyas.

Among the notable temples Pattadakal are Virupakasha Temple, Mallikarjuna Temple and Sangameshvara Temple, which shows the climax of evolution of the early Dravidian vimana style started at Aihole.

BADAMI

Southwest of Pattadakal on the Malprabha river is Badami. In the earlier texts it is mentioned as Vatapi. It was the capital of the legendary Puru Pulkesin II of the Chalukya dynasty between 543-757. Later Pallavas occupied it in the mid- seventh century finally the Rashtrakutas took over. This sleepy town is attractively situated at the mouth of a narrow valley between two rocky hills and nestling in its fold is the picturesque Bhoothnath Lake. This idyllic setting is punctuated with ruins of the fabulous golden coloured sandstone temples. The Early Chalukyas chose the finely grained horizontally stratified cliff face which facilitated excavation of large cave temples and execution of fine sculptures and intricate carvings in them. There are four such cave temples, three are Brahmanical and fourth is Jain.

Cave number three is the oldest and largest. It is dedicated to Vishnu and was excavated in 578 by king Mangalesha. The other cave is dedicated to Shiva and smaller one dedicated to Vishnu. The cave temples consist of a rectangular-pillared verandah, a square-pillared hall and a square-shrine cell in the rear. The verandahs are adorned with elaborately carved columns and the walls are decorated with life-size friezes of Hindu epics. The fourth cave temple is dedicated to Jain tirthankar, Parshwanatha. It is right on the top of the three caves and was built about a century later. It also offers a stunning view of the valley, especially that of Bhoothnath Temple on the edge of the lake whose water is said to have healing properties.

Aihole and Pattadakal are the evolution ground of the temple architecture in India, here one can
see the prototype of Dravida style in Sangameshvara Temple at Pattadakal
(Opposite page) Stone chariot in the Vitthala Temple Complex is the marvel of the Vijayanagara sculptors that remains unmatched in the country
(Previous page) For a few moments in the morning, the pavilion of Monolithic Ganesha temple at Hampi, is bathed in the golden light of sun

The door of a spice warehouse is sealed during the treatment of ginger, Jew Town, Cochin